The booklet, The Supremacy of Christ Shepherd, by William McCarrell, has found a place in many hearts; we have personally given out copies in our shepherding and grace ministry. First presented as radio messages that drew on McCarrell's vast knowledge of authors who preceded him, McCarrell's explanations have planted seeds, bearing much fruit for the glory of God. McCarrell clarifies that those who receive Jesus as Savior (the Good Shepherd) also find that He becomes their Great Shepherd who "equip[s] you in every good thing to do His will, working in us that which is pleasing in His sight, through Jesus Christ, to Him be the glory forever and ever. Amen." (Heb. 13:20-21).

—Dottie Connor-Bingham
Founder, Shepherding Grace

It's been said that meditating on Scripture is chewing on the inspired words like a cow works over its cud. William McCarrell shows us what it's like to meditate on Psalm 23 and the meaning of the "Great Shepherd" metaphor. He shows us how much there is to gain from one passage of Scripture!

—Marshall Shelley
Director of the Doctor of Ministry program
Denver Seminary

The Supremacy of Christ

Shepherd

The Supremacy of Christ
Shepherd

Dr. William McCarrell
Rev. Richard McCarrell D.D.

Grace Acres Press
Larkspur, CO

Grace Acres Press
PO Box 22
Larkspur, CO 80118
www.GraceAcresPress.com

Copyright © 2017 by Grace Acres Press. All rights reserved.

This booklet is a compilation of a series of expository messages on Psalm 23 as delivered by Dr. McCarrell on Cicero Bible Church's "On Wings of Song" broadcast. Originally published by Brown Gold Publications.

Printed in United States of America
20 19 18 17   01 02 03 04 05 06 07 08 09

All Bible references are from the King James Version unless otherwise noted.
No part of this publication may be reproduced, stored in a retrieval system, or transmitted in any form or by any means, electronic, mechanical, photocopying, recording, scanning, or otherwise, except as permitted by law, without the prior written permission of the Publisher.

Grace Acres Press also publishes books in a variety of electronic formats. Some content that appears in print may not be available in electronic books.

ISBN 978-1-60265-042-8
eBook ISBN 978-1-60265-047-3

Library of Congress Cataloging-in-Publication Data
   Names: McCarrell, William, author.
   Title: The supremacy of Christ : shepherd / William McCarrell, D.D.
   Other titles: Shepherd
   Description: Larkspur : Grace Acres Press, 2017. | "This booklet is a compilation of a series of expository messages on Psalm 23 as delivered by Dr. McCarrell on Cicero Bible Church's "On Wings of Song" broadcast. Originally published by Brown Gold Publications." | Description based on print version record and CIP data provided by publisher; resource not viewed.
   Identifiers: LCCN 2016052153 (print) | LCCN 2016040935 (ebook) | ISBN 9781602650473 | ISBN 9781602650428
   Subjects: LCSH: Bible. Psalms, XXIII--Sermons. | Shepherds in the Bible--Sermons.
   Classification: LCC BS1450 23rd (print) | LCC BS1450 23rd .M33 2017 (ebook) | DDC 252--dc23
   LC record available at https://lccn.loc.gov/2016052153

Contents

Foreword ix
Preface xi
Possession 1
Position 7
Promise 15
Progress 23
Provision 31
Prospect 37
Plentitude 45
Study Questions 53
Study Answers 57
The Authors 61

Foreword

The Twenty-Third Psalm is a rare jewel, positioned between Psalm 22, speaking of the death of Christ; and Psalm 24, picturing Christ as the triumphant King.

Dr. William McCarrell summarizes the psalm in these words: "Its compactness in content, grandeur of scope, and majesty of phraseology evidence wisdom that is supernatural." He goes on to say, "Though read, studied, memorized, quoted, preached upon, and taught for three thousand years by many millions of individuals, its freshness, fragrance, and fruitfulness increase with time."

In his lifetime, William McCarrell was a tireless preacher of the Word of God, not only in his own church, the Cicero Bible Church, but also in Bible classes in Michigan, Illinois, and Wisconsin. He was an effective soul winner who led thousands of people to Christ, including this writer as a teenager.

His exposition of Scripture finds in this psalm a summary of the Christian faith and its theology, experience, and hope. What John 3:16 is for the New Testament, Psalm 23 is for the Old Testament. A careful reading of this psalm will enrich the reader's faith, knowledge of truth, and glorious hope centered, as this is, on the Great Shepherd.

JOHN F. WALVOORD
Dallas Theological Seminary

Preface

The mental imagery upon reading the phrase "play ball" brings a smile to many a face. Due to its prominence in our culture—its historical development as well as traditions passed down from previous generations—baseball has rightly been called America's pastime. But can you imagine what it would be like to attend a baseball game played without the baseball? Watching the players stand in the field, running the bases, or swinging the bats would be pointless without the baseball. The baseball is the central component of the game.

Or try explaining to a fan in our country how American football differs from European football (soccer) without using an actual football. Frustrating, confusing, pointless: for, again, the central component in understanding each of these games is the specific ball used.

This principle is clearly understood in the sports arena but forgotten in the religious arena. In what might be the greatest days of opportunity for the church, we have departed from Christ as the central component of our preaching and embraced sermons of self-actualization and positive pep talks. In other words, we are trying to play the game without the ball.

What is needed is a *greater* focus on Christ rather than a diminishing focus. As the Apostle Paul opens the eighth chapter of Romans, he declares, "There is no condemnation for those in Christ Jesus." One of the great apostle's favorite phrases for a believer is "in Christ."

But if we as believers fail to fully comprehend the central component of what this means, we will fail to fully and practically appreciate all we positionally possess in Christ. It would be like buying a new car and using only a fraction of the options available because we fail to read the owner's manual.

Nor are we free to develop our own concept of Christ. This would be like allowing participants in the baseball game to develop their own baseball. The pitchers would want them small and the batters would want them fat—impossibilities if the game is going to make sense.

Today, if the church is going to make sense as true light in the midst of darkness, we must lift up Christ. Not our own ideas concerning Christ, but the true Christ who declared in the Bible (John 14:6): "I am the way, the truth, the life."

When this Christ came into our world as Saviour, He was more than just a man. He was and remains today the God-Man. In Christ the Godhead took on flesh (John 1:1 14). God is truth; thus, this Christ who is God Incarnate can say "I am the Truth." He lived a sinless life and in fact as God was sinless (II Cor. 5:21), so when He died on the cross, it was not deserved payment for His own sin. Therefore, He was able to die as our substitute, for *our* sin. God is holy and demands full payment for sin. Because Jesus Christ died as our substitute for our sin, He can rightfully say "I am the Way," for He alone has opened the path for us into the presence of a Holy God, as we accept, by faith belief, His payment for sin. Finally, after three days, this Jesus Christ rose again in victory over death. This has been called the most substantiated event in religious history. Therefore, this Saviour, Jesus Christ, can rightfully claim that He "is the Life."

This is the Light, Life, and Hope we need to be sharing with a spiritually dark and hopeless world. This changeless, consistent Christ must be the central component of all we do and say.

Some years ago my grandfather authored a series of booklets on various aspects of the ministry of this Saviour, whose arrival and ministry were prophesied in the Old Testament and recorded in the New Testament Gospels, and whose return is the focus of the New Testament epistles.

I am reprinting them to encourage those of us who have come to embrace Him by faith as our Saviour to walk in the fullness of all He brings to our lives. In these five booklets, we see the Lord Jesus Christ as our: ***Shepherd***, from the words of David in Psalm 23; as our ***Saviour***, in all He accomplished on the cross revealed in His seven proclamations from the cross; as our *Sufficiency*, as we view the treasures we possess on account of His resurrection; as our *Security*, as we meditate on our position in Christ shared in the words of Romans chapter 8; and finally, as our *Satisfaction*, by examining the words and warnings of Christ's seven letters to the church contained in Revelation chapters 2 and 3.

May these be a great encouragement to all who read them.

Because of Christ Alone,
Rev. Rich McCarrell, D.D.

Chapter 1

Possession

Psalm 23 nestles in the midst of three significant psalms. Psalm 22 describes Jesus Christ as a Saviour dying on the **cross**. Psalm 23 presents Him as a resurrected **Shepherd** with power for saved ones. Psalm 24 presents Him as a **King** with triumphant glory to be shared by His children. In these Psalms faith sees a cross, a shepherd's crook, and a crown. Psalm 22 emphasized the **cross** upon which Jesus died to provide salvation for His sheep. Psalm 23 emphasizes the shepherd's **crook** with which Jesus rests, strengthens, and assists His sheep. Psalm 24 emphasizes the **crown** which assures Jesus' triumphant glory and is to be shared by His sheep.

The Bible presents the Lord Jesus Christ in a three-fold shepherd aspect: the **Good**, the **Great**, and the **Chief Shepherd**. In John 10:11 Jesus declares, "I am the **Good** Shepherd: the **Good** Shepherd giveth His life for the sheep." Here Jesus is the Good Shepherd **dying** for His sheep. In Hebrews 13:20 God says, "Now the God of peace, that brought again from the dead our Lord Jesus, that **Great** Shepherd of the sheep, through the blood of the everlasting covenant." Here Scripture declares that Jesus in resurrection power is acting as the

Great Shepherd in keeping His sheep. In I Peter 5:4 the Spirit states, "And when the chief Shepherd shall appear, ye shall receive a crown of glory that fadeth not away." Here the Lord Jesus is referred to as the **Chief** Shepherd, who is **coming** a second time for His sheep. His death as the Good Shepherd is a **past** work through which He provides a past salvation from the penalty of sin (I Timothy 2:9; Ephesians 2:5-8). In His resurrected, crucified body as the **Great** Shepherd of His sheep, He now makes possible moment-by-moment victory over the power of sin. This **present** work provides a present, moment-by-moment salvation from the power of sin (Philippians 2:12, 13; Romans 8:2; Galatians 2:19, 20). Jesus is coming as the **Chief** Shepherd to **deliver** and glorify His sheep. This **coming** work provides a future salvation from the presence of sin (Romans 13:11; I Peter 1:5; I John 3:2).

In the Bible, God's children are His saved ones and referred to as His "sheep." Scripture states that God "made his own people to go forth like sheep, and guided them in the wilderness like a flock" (Psalm 78:52). Also, "so we thy people and sheep of thy pasture will give thee thanks for ever" (Psalm 79:13). Jesus, referring to saved ones, said, "My sheep hear my voice, and I know them, and they follow me: and I give unto them eternal life; and they shall never perish, neither shall any man pluck them out of my hand" (John 10:27, 28).

Psalm 23 magnifies the work of the Lord Jesus Christ for saved ones during their pilgrimage on earth. This wondrous psalm is referred to as a "song out of the night," the echoes of which infiltrate deepest darkness with hope of brightest dawn. It has been likened to a string of pearls brought up from the depths of human sorrow, trouble, need, and fear; and pearls that are made to shine through truth concerning the reason for Lord Jesus and His victory over the grave. Another likened this psalm to a golden harp with every verse a crystal chord. Human faith can bring from each chord heavenly music, especially for those in Christ—music which the unsaved world knows nothing of.

I am confident that Psalm 23 ranks with John 3:16 and John 14:1-6 as the most frequently quoted portions of Scripture. Many Christian servants believe it has been heard in more death chambers and funeral services than any other part of God's Word. God alone can correctly estimate the comfort brought during sad and trying circumstances; and more than that, the salvation wrought amongst mankind through this psalm. Its beginning assures God's child of the supply of every need.

The saved one then glides along with the Lord presented as everything needed for every test and experience during life on earth. In closing, the psalm pictures the end of a believer's physical life. At such a time, death flees from them! Shadows dissolve before them! Gates of glory open to them! The heavenly home awaits them! And finally, eternal bliss is forever more enjoyed by them! In its beginning, Psalm 23 enable every Christian to calmly and victoriously face every need and trial in life with the assuring conviction, "I shall not want." Later, when facing death, the same believer triumphantly declares, "I will dwell in the house of the Lord forever."

Verse 1 of Psalm 23 reads:

The Lord is my shepherd; I shall not want.

Five words in the verse so describe the Shepherd as to assure wondrous blessings through Him. The Shepherd is identified by the word "Lord." The identification assures every saved one of the deity of their Shepherd. Being divine, He is supernatural, perfect, and miraculous. He is a Shepherd whose preciousness, ability, faithfulness, greatness, and love cannot be surpassed nor supplanted. When God said to Abraham, "I am thy shield" (Genesis 15:1), He assured Abraham that he could possess no greater shield for safety. This psalm teaches that the most timorous believer in Jesus Christ as Saviour can say, "The Lord is my shepherd." There can be none greater.

The word "Lord" also assures that every believer possesses an omnipotent, omniscient, and omnipresent Shepherd. It was after His bodily resurrection and before His ascension in that resurrected, crucified body to the right hand of God to live as a caretaker for His sheep, that Jesus said, "All power is given unto me in heaven and in earth" (Matthew 28:18). Every Christian possesses this supernatural, divine, and abundantly sufficient Shepherd: a Shepherd who can easily solve every problem, carry every burden, give victory over every temptation, bridge every chasm, overcome every enemy, and carry to glory.

The short word "is" offers abundance of comforting truth. It assures saved ones that the omnipresent Lord is their **present** Shepherd. The oriental shepherd guides, provides for, and protects his sheep with his very person. He does this because he is a true shepherd. Every good thing a human shepherd does or is for his sheep illustrates that which Christ does and is for His sheep. One becomes His sheep by coming unto God through Him.

The words "not want" in this first verse assure a **sufficient** Shepherd. Everyone possessing Jesus Christ, the sufficient Shepherd, shall have every need supplied. "**Not want**" means they shall **not be without**. Why should they be without when in Christ Jesus, the Shepherd, resides all power (Matthew 28:18); also all treasures of wisdom and knowledge (Colossians 2:3)? Scripture declares that in Him dwelleth all fullness (Colossians 1:19); yes, even the fullness of the Godhead bodily (Colossians 2:9). These portions of God's Word teach that all that God, Christ, or the Holy Spirit ever have been, all they now are, and all they ever will be is resident in the Lord Jesus Christ. Through Him God can and does supply a Christian's every need (Philippians 4:19). The assurance of **"not want"** unlocks Psalm 23. The saved one can say:

I shall not want **rest**	because "**He** maketh me to lie down in green pastures."
I shall not want **refreshment**	because "**he** leadeth me beside … still waters."
I shall not want **forgiveness**	because "**He** restoreth my soul."
I shall not want **companionship**	because "though I walk through the valley of the shadow of death, … **thou** art with me."
I shall not want **comfort**	because "**thy** rod and **thy** staff they comfort me."
I shall not want **food**	because "**Thou** preparest a table before me in the presence of mine enemies."
I shall not want the **Holy Spirit**	because "**thou** anointest my head with oil."
I shall not want **satisfaction**	because "my cup runneth over."
I shall not want **any good thing**	because "goodness and mercy shall follow me all the days of my life."
I shall not want **anything** in **eternity**	because "I will dwell in the house of the Lord forever."

No wonder a little girl, with a great faith, said in quoting this verse, "The Lord is my Shepherd, I shall not worry."

In a certain sense, the most vital word to the reader in this first verse of Psalm 23—yea, possibly the most vital word in the entire psalm—is a short but significant word of two letters; it spells "my." It indicates a **personal** Saviour and Shepherd; it assures personal possession. In Psalm 62 the same word is used in the same comforting sense. It is a testimony that every saved one can share. Here, David, through God's Spirit, testifies that God is "my Rock, my Fortress, my Deliverer, my God, my strength, my Buckler, my Salvation, and my High Tower." The "my shepherd" of Psalm 23 includes all and more than that assured by the word "my" in Psalm 62. How precious and important this word "my" is! If one cannot say, "He is **my** Shepherd," they cannot claim even one of the many blessings enumerated in this Twenty-third Psalm.

A little lad had a pocket knife. As his friends gathered about him, one said, "It has a corkscrew." He said, "It is mine!" Another said, "It has a pearl handle." He replied, "It is mine!" Another said, "It has six blades." He exclaimed, "It is mine." It is so wonderful to be able to say of Christ, "My beloved is mine and I am his" (Song of Solomon 2:16)!

One will never have Jesus Christ as Shepherd unless they receive Him as Saviour. Scripture assures that whosoever will may receive Him as Saviour. A man bound by sin was handed a Gospel of John while plowing in a field. Sitting by the fence, he read, "For God so loved the world, that he gave his only begotten Son, that whosoever believeth in him should not perish, but have everlasting life" (John 3:16). He said, "It is wonderful that God loved the world; I can understand that. It is wonderful that He gave His Son; I can understand that. It is wonderful that whosoever believes in His Son will not perish but have everlasting life—but I wonder who God means by 'whosoever'?" He called a little lad, on his way to school, over to the fence, and reading the verse said, "Sonny, do you know who 'whosoever' means?" The little boy, standing there with his school books, thought a while and said, "It must mean you, me, or anyone else." The boy was correct. The man grasped the truth, received Jesus as Saviour by faith, and was born again of God's Spirit.

A young fellow lay dying, and with sight going said, "Mother, read John 3:16 to me and as you do, place my finger upon the word 'whosoever.'" He thus expressed his faith in Christ as Saviour. As Saviour, Jesus would make real to him, as He does to every saved one, all the work of the Shepherd described in Psalm 23.

This psalm offers wonderful blessing to everyone who hears, reads, or studies it. One saved through a radio message (preached by me) later heard me speak on this Twenty-third Psalm. She sent a card with the following testimony:

> With me—my Shepherd
> Beneath me—green pastures
> Beside me—still waters
> Upon me—anointing oil
> After me—goodness and mercy
> Beyond me—the house of the Lord.

Chapter 2

Position

Psalm 23 was spoken by God's Spirit through David three thousand years ago. During these many centuries, it has rested the weary; brought peace to the perplexed; comforted the sorrowing, overcome grief, healed the broken-hearted; liberated captives to circumstances, self, and sin; strengthened the weak; encouraged the discouraged; made bold the timid; removed the fear of death, prepared for heaven, and equipped the Christian warrior. These blessings have been imparted worldwide and to such numbers of mankind as reach beyond human estimation. It still lives! Each verse adds to the number of comforting blessings, and opportunities for spiritual enrichment, which the psalm offers believers. Its values increase with time. In every generation it serves as a vehicle for expressing unnumbered testimonies by Christians, and will continue to so serve until every Christian enters the presence of the Saviour and Shepherd whom it describes.

This psalm has been called "the nightingale song" because the nightingale sings in the night and its song becomes sweeter as the night deepens. Just so the comfort and richness of Psalm 23 increase as shadows, trials, and darkness deepen. One described how, while standing at the open grave of his mother, a singing meadowlark ascended out of the grass nearby. Its song increased in volume and sweetness as it ascended in height. Some have named this psalm "the meadowlark song" because of conviction that experience of its richness is proportioned by one living above earthly things and in the heavenlies.

Psalm 22 stands as a great mountain peak describing Jesus Christ as the Good Shepherd (John 10:11). Here faith sees Him a **Sacrificial Shepherd** dying for His sheep in order to secure God's multiplied, even eternal, blessings for them. Psalm 24 stands as an opposite mountain peak. It describes Jesus Christ as the **Chief Shepherd**, a **Rewarding Shepherd** who at His coming will culminate the blessings the **Good Shepherd** secured for God's sheep. Psalm 23 stands as a valley between these peaks. It describes Jesus Christ as the **Great Shepherd**, a keeping Shepherd, one who with all power lives in His resurrected, crucified body to keep His sheep moment by moment. So doing, He makes real in daily life the blessings secured by the **Good Shepherd's** death and consummated at the **Chief Shepherd's** return.

Psalm 23 can be likened unto a rich, fragrant, fruitful, refreshing, and restful valley nestling between these two peaks: A valley with singing brooks and streams amongst high hills and rugged rocks, and offering refreshing waters for weary wayfarers. Its green pastures and still waters illustrate rest experienced by limpid lakes and in green glens, also shelter from burning sun through shade of overhanging rocks. Its closing reference to the Lord's house suggests the protection, provision, and rest at close of day experienced through precious home life and its multiplied blessings.

Verse 2 of Psalm 23 reads:

> "**He** *maketh* **me** *to lie down in green pastures:* **he** *leadeth* **me** *beside the still waters."*

The first word of verse 2 is "He." It assuringly reminds that the blessings of verse 2, as well as those of the entire psalm, are possible because saved ones, as assured in verse 1, possess the Lord as their Shepherd. All is possible through the work of this divine, omnipotent, omniscient, omnipresent, perfect, present, and personal Shepherd. Apart from Him none of these blessings can be experienced.

In this second verse, He maketh His sheep to lie down. He does so to make sure His sheep do not miss the green pasture blessings by passing through them. *Lying* suggests the opposite of quick, hasty, surface experience. This position speaks of humiliation. It suggests saying nothing, doing nothing, and being nothing before the Shepherd. It acknowledges helplessness before Him and utter dependence upon Him. The word "maketh" teaches that this wondrous Shepherd serves as guide, guardian, director, also ruler of His sheep. He maketh His own to lie down through various means. At times they lie down because He has so attracted—yea, captivated—them by His love, preciousness, and grace that they are lost in Him, and yearningly hunger for His presence. They say:

> *I have a Friend so precious,*
>   *So very dear to me,*
> *He loves me with such tender love,*
>   *He loves so faithfully,*
> *I could not live apart from Him.*
>   *I love to feel Him nigh;*
> *And so we dwell together,*
>   *My Lord and I.*
>
> ("My Lord and I," Lancaster, 1890)

At times the Shepherd forces His sheep to lie down through trial, upset, even suffering. In such instances, He desires to make "all things work together for good to them that love God, to them who are called according to his purpose" (Romans 8:28). He often makes Himself more real and precious through a lying-down experience. David testified, "Before I was afflicted I went astray: but now have I kept thy word. It is good for me that I have been afflicted; that I might learn thy statutes" (Psalm 119:67, 71).

Some describe how a shepherd occasionally breaks the leg of a lamb, that through timidity or stubbornness has persistently refused his offers of help, and then tenderly resets the broken limb. During the period of helplessness and convalescence, the shepherd, by his care, so convinces the lamb of his love as to draw it to himself. It has been said that such a lamb will then surpass others of the flock in dependence upon, devotion to, and close following of the shepherd.

An exceptionally active preacher was set aside for a time through illness. He told a visiting preacher that he could not understand why he should be made inactive while speaking so much for God. The visiting preacher, agreeing that he had been much occupied with speaking for God, suggested that possibly God laid him aside in order to get a chance to speak to him, and thus better equip him to do better speaking for God.

The words "**lie down**" suggest opportunity for one to listen, ponder, take inventory, and learn.

The Shepherd makes His sheep to lie down in green pastures. Green pastures are filled with grass that is attractive, restful, and budding with life. Such pastures are rare; they are sheltered spots, usually hidden away from traveled highways, especially in a mountainous, hilly country such as Palestine; pastures not burnt by the warm sun, nor ruined through trampling of feet. A green pasture speaks of rest; green is the most restful color known to mankind. It is the only color that the human eye can gaze upon continually without becoming wearied. The shepherd would have to know the location of such pastures. It is his work to select them for the sheep, as well as to lead the sheep into them. He will always select the best. He makes the sheep to lie down in the pasture, not only in order that they be strengthened through feeding, but also that they benefit by digestion. Lying down, the sheep chews its cud and properly digests the food eaten.

Green pastures, teeming with nourishment, illustrate continuous and rich spiritual sustenance. God desires that believers do not live upon stale, past blessings, but continually enjoy new spiritually enriching experiences. The Saviour who has provided eternal and glorified life for believers, now as their Great Shepherd desires to so lead them as to enable them to experience life more abundant (John 10:10). They will experience life abundant as they appropriate spiritual blessings and enrichment through reading, meditating, studying, and obeying God's Word. Jeremiah testified: "Thy words were found, and I did eat them; and thy Word was unto me the joy and rejoicing of mine heart" (Jeremiah 15:16). Lying down in green pastures illustrates a Christian's steadfast, continual living in God's Word.

The saved one's Shepherd leads His sheep beside still waters. Sheep need a leader. Scripture states: "O LORD, I know that the way of man is not in himself; it is not in man that walketh to direct his steps" (Jeremiah 10:23). In His omniscience, He never guides wrong. God through Isaiah says: "I am the LORD thy God which teacheth thee to profit, which leadeth thee by the way that thou shouldst go" (Isaiah 48:17). Jesus, referring to Himself as Shepherd, said, "And when he putteth forth his own sheep, he goeth before them, and the sheep follow him: for they know his voice" (John 10:4).

Jesus Christ desires to lead and not force; He always leads His sheep for their good. He loves to lead them by His Spirit enlightening through God's Word. He may be forced to lead through gentle pressure or by the chastening rod. Such means are used when His leading by the Spirit through the Bible is not followed. God, through the psalmist, says: "I will instruct thee and teach thee in the way which thou shalt go: I will guide thee with mine eye. Be ye not as the horse, or as the mule, which have no understanding: whose mouth must be held in with bit and bridle" (Psalm 32:8, 9).

"**Still waters**" speak of separation from this world's turmoils and distractions; they speak of secret fellowship with God. "He that dwelleth in the secret place of the most High shall abide under the shadow of the Almighty" (Psalm 91:1). They suggest times of quietness and thoughtfulness; periods not characterized by the noise of the eagle, but rather by the quietness of the dove; not as the wind of the hurricane, but as the quiet refreshment of the dew. Still waters suggest nourishment, refreshment, and cleansing. They illustrate spiritual rest in Jesus, who said, "Come unto me, all ye that labour and are heavy laden, and I will give you rest" (Matthew 11:28).

Turbulent waters are invariably shallow; sheep do not drink of them. Sheep drink of still waters. Thus doing, they partake of the best and safest. They can detect anything dangerous to drink in the still, transparent waters, but this would not be true of the turbulent. These waters illustrate the life meant by Jesus when He said, "the water that I shall give him shall be in him a well of water springing up into everlasting life" (John 4:14); also, "He that believeth on Me, as the Scripture hath said, from within him shall flow rivers of living water" (John 7:38 R.V.).

In this precious verse 2 of Psalm 23, the Shepherd places His sheep in green pastures to feed them. After partaking of His provision, they are responsive to His leadership and are guided into richer blessing. In spiritual life, the Christian who is strengthened by partaking of God's provision, through living in God's word, will yield to further guidance by Jesus Christ. He, the divine and Great Shepherd, will guide them beside still waters for meditation, inventory, rest, and strengthening. He yearns to so guide in their thoughts, words, plans, and service as to make them His *very own* through them.

Verse 1 of the psalm emphasizes that relationship must exist between Shepherd and sheep if one is to experience the blessings described in this rich Scripture portion. The individual must be able to say, "The LORD is **my** Shepherd." The same personal relationship emphasized in verse 1 by the word "my" is set forth in verse 2 by the words "He" and "me."

The one who can truthfully say, "The LORD is **my** Shepherd" can also say, "I shall not **want**." The word "want" not only suggests needs supplied, but it also implies "no want" because of complete satisfaction with that possessed and experienced. God's spiritual green pastures, which suggest His Word, and still waters, which suggest His life in and through Christ Jesus, can so strengthen, sustain, and satisfy saved ones along spiritual lines as to cause them to truthfully say:

I shall not want **rest**	because "He maketh me to lie down in green pastures."
I shall not want **refreshment**	because "he leadeth me beside the still waters."
I shall not want **restoration**	because "He restoreth my soul."
I shall not want **counsel**	because "he leadeth me in the paths of righteousness for His name's sake."
I shall not want **companionship**	because "though I walk through the valley of the shadow of death, Thou art with me."
I shall not want **comfort**	because "thy rod and thy staff they comfort me."
I shall not want **provender**	because "Thou preparest a table before me in the presence of mine enemies."
I shall not want **power**	because "thou anointest my head with oil."
I shall not want **satisfaction**	because "my cup runneth over."
I shall not want **anything** here	because "goodness and mercy shall follow me all the days of my life."
I shall not want **anything hereafter**	because "I will dwell in the house of the LORD for ever."

To one with such faith, God's word assuringly replies:

Thou shalt experience rest in Jesus, who said:

"Come unto me, all ye that labor and are heavy laden, and I will give you rest" (Matthew 11:28).

Thou shalt have refreshment in Jesus, who said:
"If any man thirst, let him come unto me, and drink" (John 7:37).

Thou shalt enjoy restoration and forgiveness in Jesus, who said:
"Thy sins are forgiven" (Luke 7:48).

Thou shalt be blessed with counsel and guidance in Jesus, who said:
"I am the light of the world: he that followeth me shall not walk in darkness, but shall have the light of life" (John 8:12).

Thou shalt be enriched with companionship in Jesus, who said:
"And, lo, I am with you always, even unto the end of the world" (Matthew 28:20).

Thou shalt enjoy comfort in Jesus, who said:
"I will not leave you comfortless" (John 14:18).

Thou shalt partake of provision (food) in Jesus, who said:
"I am the bread of life: he that cometh to me shall never hunger" (John 6:35).

Thou shalt be anointed with power in Jesus, who said:
"All power is given unto me in heaven and in earth" (Matthew 28:18).

Thou shalt experience satisfaction and joy in Jesus, who said:
"These things have I spoken unto you, that my joy might remain in you, and that your joy might be full" (John 15:11).

Thou shalt not lack anything in this life in Jesus, who said:
"Seek ye first the kingdom of God, and his righteousness; and all these things shall be added unto you" (Matthew 6:33).

Thou shalt not be found wanting anything in eternity in Jesus, who said:
"And if I go and prepare a place for you, I will come again, and receive you unto myself; that where I am, there ye may be also (John 14:3).

A Christian traveler in Switzerland told a little Swiss shepherd boy about salvation through Jesus, the Shepherd. The little fellow could not read, so made slow work of it. The traveler finally suggested that he could remember about Jesus being his Saviour and Shepherd by using his four fingers and thumb. He said, "Take the five words, 'The Lord is my Shepherd,' one for the thumb and one for each finger." Later, traveling in the same territory, he went to the little fellow's home to learn how he was doing. The mother stated that her boy had died. He expressed his sorrow. The mother then asked, "Are you the man who taught my boy to say something on his fingers?" He replied that he was. She then said, "My boy told me that if you should come this way, to tell you that he died holding the fourth finger of his hand." This fourth finger was linked with the word "my." He meant, "The Lord is '**my**' Shepherd."

Luther said, "The richness of spiritual experience is dependent upon one appropriating that indicated in Scripture by personal and possessive pronouns." The word "**my**," when evidencing possessing Jesus Christ as Saviour, is a wonderful word to die by. However, it can also be a wonderful word to *live* by, if it indicates that one is appropriating, experiencing, and enjoying the Great Shepherd who lives for, in, and through His sheep, who are His saved ones. Such life with the Shepherd can only be enjoyed after one has become His sheep by receiving Him as Saviour.

Chapter 3

Promise

The Lord Jesus said, "Search the scriptures; for ... they are they which testify of me" (John 5:39). Scripture says that "in him [Jesus] dwelleth all the fullness of the Godhead bodily" (Colossians 2:9). When He is discerned and apprehended in Bible study, one finds all of Scripture overflowing with spiritual blessings and riches because His fullness courses through Scripture.

Study of Jesus Christ as presented in Psalms 22, 23, and 24 increases the many evidences that Jesus' statements about Himself in Scripture are true. Psalm 22 presents Him as the Good Shepherd dying on the cross for His sheep. Here His submission to shameful humiliation, even the cursed death of the cross, is emphasized. In Psalm 22 He is referred to as a "**worm**." In Psalm 23 He is presented as the resurrected Shepherd with a shepherd's **crook**. In Psalm 24 faith sees Him as the **King** of glory wearing His **crown**. The same Jesus who in Psalm 22 is described as a **worm** is described in Psalm 23 as a victorious, resurrected One aiding His people with the shepherd's **crook**. Psalm 24 then pictures Him as the **King** with a heavenly crown. This three-fold description offers saved ones unbreakable assurance of His ability, based upon His person and work, to make every blessing described in Psalm 23 real to them in time and eternity.

Verse 3 of Psalm 23 reads:

He restoreth my soul: he leadeth me in the paths of righteousness for his name's sake.

The first word, **"He,"** binds the believer to the divine, omnipotent, omniscient, omnipresent, perfect, personal, present Shepherd assured every saved one in the psalm's opening verse. This God-inspired statement through David, "He restoreth my soul," is strengthened by the fact that it also expresses David's personal experience. David knew the folly of wandering from God; also the suffering caused by it. He testified that while out of fellowship with God, his bones waxed old within him, and his moisture was turned into the drought of summer (Psalm 32:3, 4); also that the joy of the Lord had departed from him (Psalm 51:12).

God's saved ones are His sheep (John 10:15, 26-28). They became His sheep when they were saved from ruin. Sheep always need a shepherd. They can never fall away from salvation, but they can fall from fellowship with the Shepherd, even after experiencing spiritual strengthening through being fed in green pastures and rested by still waters.

God's sheep stray when they fall from fellowship with the Shepherd. When thus stumbling in their spiritual life, they lose unnumbered spiritual blessings, the Shepherd's care, and invariably suffer His chastening rod. When so straying, they experience loss of holiness, happiness, peace, prayer power, and spiritual fruitage.

How blessed for straying followers to know that their Saviour lives as their Great Shepherd, with an unchangeable love for them, and a desire to restore them. When the soul grows sorrowful, He lives to revive it; when it is sinful, He lives to sanctify it; when it is weak, He lives to strengthen it. A hymn reads:

> *Though I forsake Him and wander away;*
> *Still He doth love me wherever I stray.*
> *Back to His dead loving arms would I flee,*
> *When I remember that Jesus loves me.*
>
> ("Jesus Loves Even Me," Bliss, 1870)

Saved ones should remember that straying from fellowship with Christ, the Great Shepherd, is evidenced in Christian life whenever the following conditions exist:

1. Preferring to talk about things, events, or persons, rather than about Christ.
2. Desiring to read books about the Bible, rather than the Bible.
3. Waning interest in public worship of Christ.
4. Lack of occupancy with Christ.
5. Spiritual obedience becoming wearisome.
6. Tendency to gloss over Biblical error.
7. Avoiding responsibility in dealing with sin.
8. Lack of interest in salvation of souls.
9. Lack of interest in missionary work.
10. Being satisfied with flashy religious exterior.
11. Lack of concern over personal sin.
12. Worldliness in life.

This great **keeping** Shepherd restores, by bringing straying sheep to repentance for, and confession of, any sin that caused broken fellowship. Everything involved in restoration, such as forgiveness, cleansing, deliverance, and victory, are supplied through the restoring Saviour and Shepherd. Restoration is accompanied by renewal of prayer fellowship, interest in and obedience to God's Word, witnessing for the Saviour through victorious living and spoken word, and also by sincere desire to separate from all worldliness and known sin.

The Great Shepherd of Psalm 23 lives to lead those saved in paths of righteousness, meaning paths of rightness and right living. How comforting God's assurance, "I will instruct thee and teach thee in the way which thou shalt go: I will guide thee with mine eye" (Psalm 32:8). Also, His testimony through the psalmist, "For this God is our God for ever and ever: he will be our guide even unto death" (Psalm 48:14). Jesus Christ also assures, "I am the light of the world: he that followeth me shall not walk in darkness, but shall have the light of life" (John 8:12). The Christian who has been led by the Shepherd into the blessings of green pastures, the rest beside still waters, and the restoration of fellowship, should continually yield to leading, which means guidance, by the Great Shepherd. Such yielding is reasonable. It is necessary if one is to walk in continuous fellowship with Christ.

Christ desires that each saved one be directed in his thinking, speaking, acting, planning, and living by Himself. The One who so often blesses His followers through leading into green pastures, beside still waters, and restoring their souls, desires to so guide their lives as to keep them in the center of His will, thus continuing and increasing spiritual blessings for them. Such leading will also keep them living, shining, and fruitful for Him. Such a life will move in paths of righteousness before God, and will enjoy God's blessing. God's Word states, "For the righteous Lord loveth righteousness; his countenance doth behold the upright" (Psalm 11:7). He may lead by the words or life of other saved ones, through tracts, Christian literature, suffering, sorrow, or sermons. His chief means of leading is God's Word. He desires that it be a lamp for the feet and a light to the path of every Christian (Psalm 119:105).

Christ never leads His sheep into anything but paths of righteousness. A well-known preacher said that this statement in literal translation could read, "He leadeth me into sheep-tracks." Another Bible teacher and author interprets it, "He leadeth me in the wagon-ruts." When this psalm was written, wagon wheels were broad and caused deep ruts that aided travel. Both translations suggest that many of God's followers have traveled a similar route with safety and profit. How enlightening, heart-searching, and challenging is Jesus' statement about His sheep, which reads, "A stranger will they not follow, but will flee from him: for they know not the voice of strangers" (John 10:5).

Everyone who has become one of Christ's sheep through receiving Him as Saviour has been so led by Him as to be made righteous before God. Romans informs that every human being is without righteousness before God, declaring, "There is none righteous, **no, not one**" (Romans 3:10). It also informs that everyone is helpless as to securing righteousness through themselves or the work of man. Thus, everyone is hopeless as to ever being righteous before God through anything they or anyone can be or do. The chapter then proclaims that God, through Christ, has provided His own righteousness—yea, the very righteousness of God—for mankind (Romans 3:21-28). This righteousness is offered unto all mankind. It is placed upon all that believe; which means all that receive Jesus Christ as Saviour.

Everyone who accepts Jesus Christ as Saviour possesses God's righteousness. God's righteousness is spiritual, heavenly, perfect, and eternal, and a righteousness that cannot be improved upon by any human being, angel, seraphim, cherubim, even God Himself. It is a righteousness that is forever sufficient, that makes the believer as righteous as God, and makes them acceptable unto God in the beloved (Ephesians 1:6).

Righteousness is also used in the Bible to indicate righteous actions, meaning living which is right before God. Any word, thought, or act contrary to God's will can never be right, thus [to be righteous we] necessarily have to be in harmony with God's will. Walking in the paths of righteousness means thinking, speaking, acting, and living in the center of God's will. Living in the center of God's will is heaven upon earth for one saved, while living out of God's will is hell upon earth for them.

"**Paths of righteousness**" speak of a life characterized by prayer, obedience to God's Word, soul-winning, unyieldedness to sin, separation from worldliness, and fruitfulness in service. It is only possible as saved ones permit Christ, who is their life, to live His life in and through them. Such living tests faith. There will be experiences hard to fathom. While walking by faith, God's sheep will often see but one side. It may be a dark side. They may be tempted to question the rightness of it. However, the God who weaves their life and ever sees both sides knows all is right.

> *My life is but the weaving*
>   *Between my God and me;*
> *I may choose the colors*
>   *He weaveth steadily.*
> *Full of the weaveth sorrow,*
>   *And I in foolish pride*
> *Forget He sees the upper,*
>   *And I the under, side.*

(Author unknown)

"**Paths of righteousness**" speak of a moment-by-moment, hour-by-hour, day-by-day, year-by-year life for God. One hesitating to receive Christ as Saviour stated the fear as to not being able to live the life God desires of Christians. A Christian, holding his watch, described the tremendous task the watch had before it, in order to tick millions and millions of seconds while recording minutes, hours, then days, weeks, months, and years. He asked the hesitant one how the watch would perform such a stupendous task. He replied, "Tick after tick." The Christian reminded that just as a watch functions "tick after tick," so Jesus Christ lives His life through saved ones, even for many years, moment by moment.

The Christian's Shepherd restores the soul and leads in paths of righteousness for His Name's sake. How wonderful His Name is! Hundreds of expressions are used in God's Word to partially describe its significant richness and wonders. One verse states that, "He shall be called Wonderful, Counsellor, the mighty God, The everlasting Father, the Prince of Peace" (Isaiah 9:6). Christ promised that prayer in His Name would be answered (John 16:23). This means the petition must be presented with desire that the answer be granted only in the measure that God's will is fulfilled; also, that the petition be not granted if such would detract from God's gain, honor, or glory.

When saving Saul of Tarsus, God said that he shall bear My name (Acts 9:15). Scripture offers many indications of God's concern about His Name. Saved ones are linked with the Name of God and Christ, and His Name is linked with His honor and glory. Every Christian bears God's Name and should pray, therefore, for Thy Name's sake lead me and guide me (Psalm 31:3).

One can carry the name of another through legal process of law. A better way is to carry another's name through relationship, as a child carries the name of its father. A still better way is to carry the name of another because of the sacred bands of love, as a wife bears the name of her husband. Christians bear the name of Christ and God because of God's will and decree, also because of relationship, being children of God through faith in Christ Jesus (Galatians 3:26); and much more so because of their being part of Christ's bride and members of His body.

When saved ones live honoring His Name, the One who is named "Wonderful" will fill their lives with the wonders of His grace. He who is named "Counsellor" will so guide them as to keep them from falling, and the "everlasting Father" will enrich them through blessing of love, patience, and help associated with relationship; while He, "the Prince of Peace" whose Name they bear, will rest and enrich them with heaven's peace which passes all understanding. As they permit the Great Shepherd, Jesus Christ, to keep them in paths of righteousness for His Name's sake, they will testify:

> *I tell Him all my sorrows,*
> *I tell Him all my joys,*
> *I tell Him all that pleases me,*
> *I tell Him what annoys;*

> *He tells me what I ought to do,*
> *He tells me what to try;*
> *And do we walk together,*
> *My Lord and I.*
>
> ("My Lord and I," Lancaster, 1890)

The richness of spiritual experience often depends upon one appropriating that indicated in Scripture by personal and possessive pronouns. The chief pronouns in verse 3 of Psalm 23 are "He" and "me." They, as each other verse in the psalm, emphasize the importance of being able to truthfully say, **"The Lord is my Shepherd."**

These words "He" and "me" emphasize that all the psalm's blessings depend upon personal possession by faith of Jesus Christ as Shepherd. All God's Word teaches that such possession is impossible unless Jesus Christ is first appropriated as Saviour. Luther lacked assurance of salvation until he learned this truth. An old preacher, named David Staupitz, helped him. Staupitz reminded Luther of that article of their creed which read, "I believe in the forgiveness of sins." "Yes," answered Luther, "I believe it." "Ah!," said Staupitz, "I see what you lack. You believe in the forgiveness of David's and Peter's sins, ***but this is not enough!*** God desired that you believe that your *own* sins are forgiven." The light broke into Luther's soul, when he put **"my"** into it and thus appropriated the mercy of God in Christ (Ephesians 1:7; Psalm 23:1).

Chapter 4

Progress

Psalms 22, 23, and 24 give a composite description of Christ's Shepherd work for saved ones. Psalm 22, where the Good Shepherd is described dying for His sheep, has been referred to as "Christ's *yesterday of suffering.*" Psalm 24, where the Chief Shepherd is described in His future glory, has been referred to as "Christ's *forever of splendor.*" Psalm 23, nestling between these two wondrous psalms, and in which faith sees the Great Shepherd in resurrection power, has been referred to as "Christ's *today of grace.*" In Psalm 22 He is seen as a Saviour dying for His own; in Psalm 24, a King with glory for his own; in Psalm 23, a priest caring for His own. How wonderful to be able to say, "My beloved [Christ] *is* mine and I *am* his" (Song of Solomon 2:16).

Just as the central location of Psalm 23 suggests significant truth, so the central location of verse 4 in this same psalm offers much vital truth. Verse 1 assures that every believer possesses the Lord as their Shepherd. This possession assures the possibility of their every need being met in Him. Verse 2 assures Christians of the Shepherd's purpose to sustain them in green pastures and rest them beside still waters. Verse 3 assures of the Shepherd's ability and purpose to restore their spiritual life whenever needed, and to ever lead them in the paths of righteousness for His Name's sake. In verse 4, the saved one's Shepherd—through whom every need is met (verse 1), spiritual life strengthened (verse 2), spiritual victory maintained and the follower kept in the paths of God's righteousness while bearing His Name (verse 3)—now leads triumphantly into realms of heaven and eternal life.

Verse 4 reads:

> *Yea, though I walk through the valley of the shadow of death, I will fear no evil, for Thou art with me; Thy rod and Thy staff they comfort me.*

The first two words, "yea, though," suggest deep conviction; also unbreakable, triumphant assurance. They can be read, "yea, **although.**" The "walking through the valley of the shadow of death" suggests that which mankind often refers to as "fiery trials": experiences that test human hearts, as well as the believer's faith. God's Spirit, forewarning believers of such experiences through the Apostle Peter, says: "Beloved, think it not strange concerning the fiery trial which is to try you, as though some strange thing happened unto you: but rejoice, inasmuch as ye are partakers of Christ's sufferings; that, when his glory shall be revealed, ye may be glad also with exceeding joy" (I Peter 4:12, 13). Christians often sing:

> *When through fiery trials thy pathway shall lie,*
> *My grace, all-sufficient, shall be thy supply;*
> *The flame shall not hurt thee; I only design*
> *Thy dross to consume, and thy gold to refine.*
> ("How Firm a Foundation," Keen, ca. 1787)

The words "yea, though [or yes, although] I walk through the valley of the shadow of death, I will fear no evil," describe an experience of personal victory that unsaved individuals cannot understand nor experience. The valley begins in the death chamber, passes through the grave, and ends in heaven, the Father's house mentioned in the last verse of the psalm. The valley tests and challenges faith; the Father's house is where faith culminates in sight.

A boy was often seen happily walking through a graveyard as evening shadows fell. One asked him whether or not he became frightened during the walk. He replied, "Why should I? My home is right on the other side!"

Death for saved ones is referred to in this verse as a "shadow." In the Hebrew, the word can be translated *shade*. It is referred to as a shadow or shade in order to assure Christians that there will be no harm in it. Dogs can bite, wild beasts attack, and powerful military weapons destroy one, but their shadows cannot harm. Boys can stand beside a railroad track joyously waving their hats at passengers in a speeding train, while the shadow of the train harmlessly passes over them.

Shadows are temporary. How comforting the truth that death for saved ones, Christ's sheep, is mere shadow experience in which they do not remain. They walk through it! Walking through is evidence of life all the way. Walking through refutes any erroneous ideas or suggestions concerning soul-sleeping. God's Word says for any saved one, "to be absent from the body [is] ... to be present with the Lord" (II Corinthians 5:8). Scripture also declares, "to depart, and to be with Christ; which is far better" (Philippians 1:23).

Stephen, entering death by martyrdom, testified about the Lord Jesus standing at the right hand of God to receive him (Acts 7:54-60). These walked through death! Jesus assures every saved one of similar experience. He said, "Whosoever liveth and believeth in Me shall never die" (John 11:26). The body is the cottage of the soul and spirit. It may pass through the process of death; but the soul and spirit of every saved one, when leaving their physical body, immediately enters God's presence. There is no stopping place, not even a halfway home, on the path. Jesus said to the dying thief, "Today shalt thou be with Me in Paradise" (Luke 23:43).

Just think of stepping on shore, and finding it heaven
Of touching a hand, and finding it God's
Of breathing new air, and finding it celestial
Of waking up in Glory, and finding it "Home."
(from "Finally, Home!" Wyrtzen, 1971)

In Damascus there is a long, dark, narrow lane ending in a tunnel. A traveler descends and passes through. On the other side he emerges into the courtyard of an oriental palace, flashing with color and sunlight. A believer passes through the valley of the shadow of death into the house of the Lord to enjoy it forever.

Christ met the reality of death in order that saved ones, His sheep, might be delivered from death and experience merely its shadow. What a wonderful Saviour to make death a doorway to glory!

Christians may be tested mentally and spiritually when facing death, but faith can enable them to triumph gloriously. How blessed to remember that even dark valleys cause stars to shine more brightly. Any darkness in connection with the valley of this verse only forces followers to depend more fully upon the Shepherd, who never fails to bring them to eternal peace at the end of the testing journey. With weak or strong faith, Christians can say when entering, "O death, where is thy sting? O grave, where is thy victory?" (I Corinthians 15:55). How blessed to know that if faith is weak when entering the valley, it will be eternally triumphant after the quick passage.

The words "I will fear no evil" speak of rest, courage, and freedom from fear. Christ, the Good Shepherd, did not fear the reality of death. Christ, the Great Shepherd, has no fear in the valley of death's shadow. Millions of Christians, especially martyrs, have passed through without fear—why should God's sheep fear? God is for them, who can be against them? (Romans 8:31).

The next phrase, "for thou art with me," explains why death is but a shadow for believers, why they walk through it, also why they face it without fear. The Shepherd, who made His sheep His very own, sustained them in green pastures, rested and nourished them beside still waters, restored from all spiritual stumbling, and kept them in the paths of righteousness, now goes with His own through the shadow-valley of death.

Pastor and Mrs. P. W. Philpot, while ministering in Canada, were blessed with thirteen children. One of the little boys contracted typhoid fever after helping playmates fish out a ball that had rolled into a catch-basin. While in the contagious disease hospital and shortly before his death, Pastor Philpot called upon him. In discussing the possibility of death, the father asked the little lad whether he was afraid to go to heaven. He replied that he wasn't, but that he wished one of his brothers or sisters could go with him. What comfort to know that Jesus Christ did go with the little fellow, as He does with everyone entering the house of the Lord!

God's presence assures of all needed provision, protection, and power. David in Psalm 118:6 testified: "The LORD is on my side; I will not fear: what can man do unto me?" Again in Psalm 27:1 he said, "The LORD is my light and my salvation; whom shall I fear? The LORD is the strength of my life; of whom shall I be afraid?" Saved ones will be delivered from fear in the measure they realize the presence of the Lord Jesus. They have nothing to fear from God, for Christ has met every demand of God concerning their sin and salvation. They have nothing to fear concerning Satan, for God's Word states that "Forasmuch then as the children are partakers of flesh and blood, he [Christ, the Saviour and Shepherd] also himself likewise took part of the same; that through death he might destroy him that had the power of death, that is, the devil; and deliver them who through fear of death were all their lifetime subject to bondage" (Hebrews 2:14, 15). They have nothing to fear concerning judgment, for Jesus said, "Verily, verily, I say unto you, he that heareth My Word, and believeth Him that sent Me, hath eternal life, and cometh not into judgment, but hath passed out of death into life" (John 5:24, R.V.). They have nothing to fear concerning Christ, for He said, "All that the Father giveth me shall come to me; and him that cometh to me I will in no wise cast out" (John 6:37). Every enemy without, within, above, beneath, and around has been defeated by the saved one's wonderful Saviour. Scripture refers to this Saviour as the Shepherd who neither slumbers nor sleeps (Psalm 121:3). He accompanies saved ones through the valley of the shadow of death in order to care for every need and dispel all fear.

The noted preacher, John McNeil, told how while a young man, he returned weekends from his place of employment to his country home. It was necessary to walk a distance on a country road. One part of the road was known as dangerous because of robbers and deeds of violence committed against pedestrians. He described how on an exceptionally dark night, while walking timidly and cautiously through the dangerous area, he heard a footfall. His heart sank. Then he heard the words, "Is that you, John?" and he recognized his father's voice. His father, knowing the danger, had come in the darkness to meet and escort him. He then described how everything was brightened, every load lifted, and great relief experienced on the rest of the journey because of his father's presence.

Each saved one passing from this life to glory through the valley of the shadow of death will be met and accompanied by his Saviour. His accompanying presence will make the passage amazingly easy and triumphant. One of my close and highly esteemed friends, Brother A. F. Gaylord, business manager for so many years of the Moody Bible Institute, arrived in the presence of his Lord and Saviour a few years ago. His splendid wife sent me a copy of a poem which was read as his testimony at the services over his remains. Two of the verses read:

Did you wonder I so calmly
Trod the Valley of the Shade?
Oh! But Jesus' love illumined
Every dark and fearful glade.
And He came Himself to meet me
In that way so hard to tread;
And with Jesus' arm to lean on,
Could I have one doubt or dread?

(Author unknown)

The traveler through the valley of the shadow of death will be comforted by the same Shepherd's rod and staff that aided him during pilgrimage on earth. With the rod the shepherd defends his sheep by beating off snakes and wild beasts, even slaying them when necessary. In Matthew 4:1-11 there is a God-given account of Jesus Christ, the Saviour and Shepherd, meeting Satan, the great enemy of God's people, in combat. Jesus overcame Satan with a rod, which was the Word of God. During life on earth, the Christian will not be able to drive the devil, with his dangerous temptations, away through sincere resolutions, holy feelings, not even past heavenly experiences. They will defeat him proportionally as the Word of God, which is illustrated by the Shepherd's rod, is well known and well used.

A Christian Scotch lad confessed to his chum he was continually defeated through Satan's temptations to sin. The chum asked, "What do you do when he comes around?" The defeated boy said, "I try to sing a hymn but that does not send him away." The victorious Christian lad advised that the next time Satan tempted, his friend fight Satan with a Scripture text. He said, "He cannot stand that; that is how Jesus put him to flight" (Matthew 4:4, 7-10).

The shepherd often uses his staff to correct the sheep; especially when chastening is necessary for correction. The crook on the staff is often used to help the sheep over rocks and places where their strength is not sufficient. At times a lamb is carried in the crook of the staff. Again, it is used to check sheep when they are in danger of being injured or killed through falling off a precipice through wildness of spirit, carelessness in walk, or unconsciousness of danger. The staff with its crook frequently extricates sheep, despite temporary pain and loud protests, from hard positions which hold them helpless.

The rod and the staff offer saved ones much comfort for pilgrimage on earth, but even more for passage through the shadow of death. Spurgeon, in referring to death, said:

> *Lie still in the darkness,*
> *Sleep safe in the night,*
> *The Lord is a watchman,*
> *The Lamb is a light.*
> *Jehovah, He holdeth*
> *The sea and the land,*
> *The earth in the hollow*
> *Of His mighty hand.*
> *All's well in the darkness,*
> *All's well in the light,*
> *The Lamb is a watchman,*
> *The Lamb is a light."*
> (Author unknown, *The Century Illustrated Monthly Magazine,* vol. 1, no. 23 (1872))

One morning I was called by a preacher whose wife was in a coma. While at her bedside for prayer, she opened her eyes and noticed her five sons, husband, my brother, and myself. She sensed the significance of our being there. Looking at us, she said, "Death is not before me—death is not before me—death is not before me!" She then immediately lapsed back into the coma and slept into her Saviour's presence. A father said to his dying Christian son, "How is it now, Frank?" Frank replied, "Dad, it has been joy all the way with Christ; now it is joy overflowing!"

A father arriving home asked the reason for his wife's sorrow. She explained that their family doctor had stated that their only child, a lad of about sixteen, could not live. She said, "You will have to tell him, I cannot." Trusting Christ for grace, the father talked to his boy. The boy, sensing the situation, asked, "Dad, am I going to die?" The father tenderly asked, "Son, are you afraid to die?" The boy said, "Indeed not, I will be in heaven then, won't I, Dad?" The father assured him that he would because of his having received Jesus Christ as Saviour and trusted His shed blood and finished work on Calvary to atone for his sins. The lad then said, "Dad, do you want to know the first thing I am going to do when I get to heaven?" The father asked what he intended to do. The boy said, "I will see Jesus and tell Him that I had a dad and mother that always told me about Jesus and how to be saved through Him."

Chapter 5

Provision

A veteran preacher heard a young man preach whom he had pastored in spiritual life. The young preacher, anxious for the approval of one who had meant so much to him, asked, "What did you think of the sermon?" The old preacher said, "You did not mention Jesus Christ." The young preacher replied, "He was not mentioned in the text." The mature Bible student and pastor said, "As in England every road leads to London, so in the Bible every text leads to Jesus Christ." Jesus Christ is the root of all Bible doctrines, the certainty of all its promises, the fulfillment of all its prophecies, and the theme of each of its books. He is its one grand subject: He is the key to all Scripture.

In Psalm 22 we see Jesus Christ in His **crucifixion;** in Psalm 23 in His **resurrection,** and in Psalm 24 in His **coronation.** Each verse in Psalm 23 adds to the blessings showered through Christ upon Christians, and thus should strengthen conviction that He lives with resurrection power to be a **serving Shepherd** on their behalf. The first four verses describe His sheep, meaning saved ones, walking with Him during pilgrimage on earth, even through the valley of the shadow of death. In verse 5 we see the sheep, meaning Christians, feasting—yea, banqueting and rejoicing—because of Christ, their serving Shepherd. His preciousness increases as the journey progresses.

A significant change in personal pronouns referring to the Shepherd suggests precious truth. In the first three verses one reads: The Lord is my shepherd ... He maketh me ... He leadeth me ... for His Name's sake ... . Then suddenly the psalmist flings aside the third person and jumps to the second: I shall fear no evil, for **Thou** art with me ... Thy rod and Thy staff ... Thou preparest ... Thou anointest ... . This change in the pronoun takes place as passing through the valley of the shadow of death is considered. A close walk is suggested by the words, "Thou art with me." How like the Lord Jesus to draw His tested one nearer as shadows fall and trials arise that test faith.

Psalm 23, verse 5 reads:

Thou preparest a table before me in the presence of mine enemies: Thou anointest my head with oil; my cup runneth over.

It is significant that the prepared table, the anointing oil, and the overflowing cup follow passing through the valley of the shadow of death. This valley has been interpreted in three well-known ways. Some believe it refers to many experiences connected with one's life in this world of sin, darkness, destruction, and death. Others believe it refers to a Christian by faith reckoning himself dead in Christ unto worldliness, flesh, sin, and Satan and alive unto God, as exhorted in chapters 6 and 7 of Romans. This teaching emphasizes that Christians will experience the blessings of this verse in the measure that they believingly reckon themselves crucified, buried, and raised with Christ. The most prevalent teaching is that the valley refers to a believer passing from physical, temporal life on earth into glorified, eternal life in heaven. It is my belief that the valley refers to each of the three experiences.

God, notwithstanding unnumbered foes, sets a table for saved ones, anoints them, and causes their cup to overflow during their pilgrimage on earth. These blessings are enjoyed in greater measure as believers experience, through faith, their identification with the crucified and resurrected Christ. The blessings of this verse will surely be completely and forever experienced by saved ones in glory with their Saviour, Shepherd, and Lord.

The prepared table speaks of God's beneficent providence for His own at all times. Jesus warned about the tragedy of missing these blessings; also, that they can be missed through indifference, disobedience, rejection, rebellion, and unbelief (Matthew 22:2-14).

How sad for Christians to miss these God-offered blessings in this life! When they do so, they starve and dwarf their spiritual life and force themselves to shallow and starving experiences of living. They should profit by the experience of the prodigal son, who, coming to himself, said, "many hired servants of my father's have bread enough and to spare, and I perish with hunger!" (Luke 15:17).

The fact that God prepares a table should be sufficient incentive for everyone, especially each Christian, to partake of it. This table evidences Christ's desire to be a **serving Shepherd** unto believers. What sin to treat lightly, hinder, or thwart His desire!

The table is loaded with wondrous provision. It contains the blessings with which God daily loadeth His sheep (Psalm 68:19); also God's mercy, light, comfort, satisfaction, peace, strength, righteousness, life, salvation, sanctification, and glorification. Certainly it offers, as its bread and water, Jesus, who described Himself as the bread and water of life (John 6:35; 7:37-39). Its every detail speaks of Him—the One altogether sufficient. Sitting at the table speaks of calm, rest, satisfaction, and precious fellowship. Surely one partaking of the table would say with the psalmist, "My soul shall be satisfied as with marrow and fatness; and my mouth shall praise thee with joyful lips" (Psalm 63:5).

The words, "Thou preparest a table before me," wondrously illustrate a shepherd's work for his sheep. A Christian shepherd described how an efficient shepherd selects grazing fields for his flock. He writes that in the Holy Land, like tares among the wheat, poisonous plants continually spring up in the best sheep pastures. The roots penetrate deep in the rocky soil and their eradication has seemed impossible. Eating one of these plants can prove fatal to a sheep. The shepherd with his staff (*mettech*) precedes the flock, grubbing out every poisonous plant that he notices. He casts them on little stone pyres where, within a few hours, they are destroyed by the burning sun. In this way, he prepares a table for his sheep. If sheep do not follow close upon the shepherd, they may eat that which will cause serious sickness, even death. Many saved ones have suffered spiritual disaster through partaking of destructive error while wandering from Christ.

Sheep often feed in fields surrounded by yelping jackals, wolves, hyenas, panthers, and even lions and bears, with vulturous eagles soaring overhead. These fields may also be infested with hidden, treacherous, venomous snakes, the sting of which sometimes causes a sheep to die within an hour. Surely they eat at a table in the midst of enemies. David mentioned rescuing his sheep from the bear and the lion (I Samuel 17).

Jesus Christ lived, died, rose again, and now lives at God's right hand in order that every enemy of His followers be held off, curbed, chained, and defeated. How blessed to know that these enemies cannot prevent a saved one from partaking of God's blessings. God's table is prepared for and can be enjoyed by Christians despite every foe, including enemies that oppose before entering the valley of the shadow of death, also while passing through it. God's table will be enjoyed forever, without opposition, in heaven. What a table Peter, Paul, and Silas enjoyed while in prison (Acts 12 and 16); also the martyr Stephen while being stoned to death (Acts 7:54-60).

Each individual should ever remember that God's table is prepared for a prepared guest. One is never prepared until saved through faith in Christ's perfect, eternal work for one's sin and salvation made possible through His shed blood, death, and bodily resurrection. Christians should always remember that worldliness, selfishness, also conscious and willful sin, distract from God's table, thus preventing enjoyment and spiritual enrichment through it.

In verse 5 of Psalm 23 we read, "thou anointest my head with oil." God's anointing of His regenerated followers suggests many blessings. It often assures elevation to and equipment for an office, such as David being anointed to be king over God's people (I Samuel 13). The Bible describes the anointing of the priest for service. God anoints saved ones in order to equip them for definite service. Every saved one is anointed in order to understand and enjoy that which God has for them in Christ! Also that which He desires to perfect through them (I John 2:27). This anointing enables them to enter fellowship with the Godhead and thus enjoy the fullness of His blessing.

The anointing mentioned in this verse is followed by enjoyment of God's grace forever. Anointing of Christians with God's Spirit enables them to so abide in Him as not to be ashamed before Christ at His coming (I John 2:28). It will be consummated when they see their Saviour and forever share His likeness in glory (Ephesians 2:5-7; I John 3:2; Revelation 22:4).

The head being anointed speaks of an anointing that influences the entire being. A Christian, who for years had been a shepherd, wrote on this psalm. He describes the shepherd standing at the one entrance to the sheepfold as the sheep return for the night. He quickly but carefully examines each sheep for briars in the ears, snags in the cheeks, scratches, body bruises, or inflammation of the eyes caused by dust. Whenever such condition is found, his rod placed across the sheep's back causes it to step aside and wait until the flock has entered the fold. The shepherd then dips his hand into a bowl and tenderly, lovingly, and liberally anoints the injury with olive oil. After caressing and speaking into its uplifted face, he directs the sheep into the fold for rest.

Oil in God's Word symbolizes the Holy Spirit, the third member of the Godhead, who indwells every saved one, anoints them for special service, and fills them as they yield to Him. Jesus Christ enjoyed anointing surpassing all others (Psalm 45:7). His anointing is associated with joy and gladness (Hebrews 1:9). It can be experienced by Christians moment by moment, day by day, and year by year until they enter heaven. Oil smoothes, soothes, satisfies, and causes the face to shine. It produce freshness, fragrance, and fruitfulness. It illustrates the spiritual work which the Holy Spirit does in and through believers.

Verse 5 of Psalm 23 closes with the glorious testimony, "my cup runneth over." A cup, especially at a table, speaks of one partaking of that which contains something prepared and offered by another. Here it speaks of God's redeemed ones partaking of life filled with blessings from God through Jesus Christ, the Great Resurrected Shepherd.

The word "my" speaks of personal appropriation and experience. "Running over" speaks of fullness of blessings. It illustrates a life so blessed as to flow out to others. It describes a satisfying, enriching, joyful experience through partaking of God's blessings from His table set in the midst of enemies, even in the midst of death, which is referred to as the Christian's last great enemy (Psalm 30:5). How significant that the overflowing cup is mentioned near the close of the journey depicted in this psalm. It assures that though weeping endure for a night, joy cometh in the morning (Psalm 30:5).

The overflowing cup speaks of God's abundance for saved ones. Scripture declares that in God there is abundance of goodness and truth (Exodus 34:6); abundance of mercy (Titus 3:6); abundance of blessing (Romans 8:32); abundance of life (John 10:10); abundance of bliss and glory (Revelation 1:4, 22:4, 5); also abundance of grace through which God makes possible all blessings in time and eternity (II Corinthians 4:15; I Timothy 1:14). Through God's abundance, every Christian's cup can overflow with salvation, sanctification, satisfaction, glorification, and eternal bliss. Christians should heed Bible warning that partaking of a cup of worldliness, self, or sin will rob them of the spiritual satisfaction, enrichment, fruitfulness, and service made possible through partaking of God's cup.

Everyone unsaved should remember that Jesus drank a cup filled with suffering, shame, woe, wrath, death, and hell. He drank it in order that everyone might enjoy the cup described in this wondrous verse. God's Word warns of a cup overflowing with wrath, judgment, and eternal punishment for all who reject Jesus Christ as Saviour.

An engine driver saved from deep sin said, "The Psalmist could say, 'my cup runneth over,' but I think the Lord makes both my cup and saucer to run over." History teaches that whenever the Nile River overflows its banks, Egypt enjoys rich, life-giving harvest. The river's failure to overflow usually indicates much death through terrible famine.

Surely the prepared table, the anointing oil, and the overflowing cup assure of God's liberality. So many attempt to hoard spiritual light, blessings, and salvation riches for selfish purposes—also God-given talents, time, and means. Such practices are entirely foreign to God's will and desire. They rob Christians of God's best during life on earth and of Jesus Christ's "Well done" and reward for faithful life and service at His second coming. Christians only keep the blessings they give away during their physical life span.

Every Christian should express appreciation to God for the blessings of this wondrous verse and psalm through so appropriating them as to overflow and thus passing these blessings on to others in the Name of Jesus Christ and for the glory of God.

Chapter 6

Prospect

There are many evidences that Psalm 23 was written by God's Spirit through the psalmist. Its compactness in content, grandeur of scope, and majesty of phraseology evidence wisdom that is supernatural. Evidence of divine inspiration is strengthened by its inexhaustibleness. Though read, studied, memorized, quoted, preached upon, and taught for three thousand years by many millions of individuals, its freshness, fragrance, and fruitfulness increase with time.

This psalm of six verses contains one hundred and eighteen words. It presents a full scope of Christian life and experience in time and eternity. A grasp of this scope is aided by six words beginning with the letter "P"; they offer a cluster of "sweet Ps." They are:

POSSESSION—**Verse 1**
Possession of God as Shepherd.
POSITION—**Verse 2**
Position assuring spiritual sustenance through the Shepherd's guidance.
PROMISE—**Verse 3**
Promise assuring spiritual victory and fruitfulness in time and eternity.
PROGRESS—**Verse 4**
Progress even through the valley of the shadow of death.

PROVISION—**Verse 5**
Provision through God's table, anointing, and overflowing cup, even in the midst of enemies.
PROSPECT—**Verse 6**
Prospect of dwelling in the house of the Lord forever.

This psalm of one hundred and eighteen divinely inspired words magnifies:

RELATIONSHIP with the Godhead	**Verse 1**
GUIDANCE into continuous blessing	**Verse 2**
RESTORATION in spiritual living	**Verse 3**
RIGHTEOUSNESS in daily living and before God	**Verse 3**
COMFORT in life and death	**Verse 4**
COURAGE when passing through the valley of the shadow of death	**Verse 4**
PROVISION, SATISFACTION, and JOY notwithstanding all enemies	**Verse 5**
GOODNESS and MERCY during earthly life	**Verse 6**
BLISS forever in God's presence	**Verse 6**

Each verse in the psalm adds to the description of a saved one's blessings during pilgrimage from earth to glory. Blessings increase as the journey progresses. Assurance is given that God's people can experience that which they often express with such words as: "Sweeter as the years go by"; also, "Each day He grows still sweeter than He was the day before." The Christian who begins in verse 1 to travel by faith as a pilgrim with the Saviour and Shepherd, now in the last verse is seen a dweller in the house of the Lord forever. Such followers often sing during pilgrimage on earth:

> *E'en down to old age all my people shall prove*
> *My sovereign, eternal, unchangeable love,*
> *And then, when gray hairs shall their temples adorn,*
> *Like lambs they shall still in my bosom be borne.*
> ("How Firm a Foundation," Keen, 1787)

In the house of the Lord they shall forever sing with spirit and meaning made new through experience:

> *The soul that on Jesus hath leaned for repose,*
> *He will not, He will not desert to its foes,*

> *That soul, tho' all hell should endeavor to shake,*
> *He'll never, no never, no never forsake!*
> ("How Firm a Foundation," Keen, 1787)

Verse 6 of Psalm 23 reads:

> *Surely goodness and mercy shall follow me all the days of my life: and I will dwell in the house of the L*ORD *forever.*

The first word, "**surely**," indicates assurance of blessing throughout Christian experience on earth and, even more, assurance of eternal salvation in glory. This assurance is strengthened by reviewing God's blessings since possessing the Great Shepherd, Jesus Christ. It produces conviction and testimony that God's goodness and mercy have permeated every phase of one's life with God. Some have referred to these two blessings as two angels which accompany God's sheep. One writer likens them to the shepherd's faithful dogs that attend and guard the sheep as they follow their shepherd.

God's goodness includes unnumbered blessings with which He daily loadeth His own (Psalm 68:19). God's mercy includes His forgiveness, salvation, spiritual restorations, also victorious life and fruitful service for Christ. These blessings will be experienced in the measure that one accepts God's grace and follows Jesus Christ the Great Shepherd. They permeate a saved one's earthly life, including childhood, youth, and old age; days past, day present, and days to come; also experiences of sorrow, joy, burden, or blessing. The saved one in glory, no longer seeing through a glass darkly and no longer knowing in part, but now knowing in full (I Corinthians 13:12), realizes with new conviction that "all things work together for good to them that love God, to them who are the called according to his purpose" (Romans 8:28). This conviction will be forever strengthened by their seeing how goodness and mercy followed them all the days of their life.

Reviewing past functioning of God's grace strengthens assurance of its endless continuance. Every past Christian experience while following the Shepherd strengthens faith in the certainty of God's promises for the future, His eternal faithfulness, and also His determination that the good work which He has begun in believers will be carried on until the day of Jesus Christ (Philippians 1:6). In God's eternal home, glorified believers will exultingly testify that:

> *It is all of grace,*
> *A gift we take;*
> *Which God bestows,*
> *For Jesus' sake.*
>
> (Author unknown)

The psalm closes with the words, "I will dwell in the house of the LORD forever." This statement offers no ground for doubt regarding a saved one's eternal security and enjoyment of eternal life, bliss, and glory. The words **"I will"** rebuke all doubt, mere hoping or guessing, regarding a saved one living forever with God. My friend, Pastor Walter Knight, suggests that such assurance is reasonable because the saved one has a Shepherd who goes before His sheep (John 10:4); also a Shepherd who encampeth round about His sheep (Psalm 34:7); a Shepherd who is beneath His sheep with His everlasting arms (Deuteronomy 33:27); also a Shepherd who lives within His sheep by the indwelling Holy Spirit (John 14:16-18); even a Shepherd who travels behind His sheep with goodness and mercy. To these assurances, I add a Shepherd who is above His sheep; One who died, rose from the dead, ascended to heaven, and ever lives before God on their behalf: all this in order that they might never be condemned (Romans 8:34).

Psalm 23 climaxes with the believer dwelling in the house of the Lord forever. It is the grandest climax possible for any human being to experience. This blessing transcends all others! Whenever grasped by faith, it melts hearts cold and indifferent toward God, softens those hardened in sin, inspires believers to heavenly living, and moves followers to desire God's best. The preparation and offer of it to mankind evidence God's love. God-blessed earthly homes are but miniature illustrations of it. The heavenly home surpasses the rich preciousness of earthly homes in measure beyond human comprehension. Those already there strengthened its preciousness. This preciousness is increased by its impregnability against invasion of sickness, pain, sorrow, or death.

Eternal life in God's heavenly home will satisfy beyond measure all the yearnings those who have followed the Shepherd have had for it. The foretastes of glory experienced during sheep and shepherd days on earth will be culminated in indescribable completion and fullness. The groanings experienced in these earthly, bodily tabernacles will be forever relieved as God's own dwell there in bodies not made with hands

(II Corinthians 5:1). Every inhabitant will be glorified. The psalmist, yearning for this experience, said, "One thing have I desired of the LORD, that will I seek after; that I may dwell in the house of the LORD" (Psalm 27:4). His longing will be fully understood by every inhabitant because of dwelling in their Father's house. How blessed when everyone who has been homesick for heaven will be in heaven. One wrote: "Blessed are the homesick for heaven, for they shall reach heaven."

This psalm contains twenty-seven personal pronouns, such as I's, my's, me's, he's, thou's, thy's, and his. They are as hooks of steel which inseparably bind God's sheep, meaning saved ones, with God's Shepherd and Saviour, and consequently with all the blessings presented in this wondrous psalm. However, these pronouns challengingly present a solemn condition. One cannot be a sheep with the Lord as Shepherd **unless** they receive Jesus as Saviour. To be fed in green pastures and rested by still waters, sheep must follow the Shepherd. Spiritual victory for the sheep is conditioned upon faithful following of the Shepherd. To dwell in God's house on high, one must walk through the valley of the shadow of death. God's prepared table will only be enjoyed by prepared guests. Goodness and mercy shall **only** follow where grace and salvation lead. To dwell with God in eternity, one must, in faith, begin as a pilgrim with Him during life on earth.

Not one of Jesus' Shepherd blessings can be enjoyed unless the individual has by faith received this same Jesus as Saviour. The link of genuine salvation is necessary in order to enjoy the overwhelming flood of God's blessings. One so linked can truthfully say:

My Shepherd	"Jehovah is my Shepherd."
My Sufficiency	"I shall not want."
My Repose	"He maketh me to lie down in green pastures."
My Refreshment	"He leadeth me beside still waters."
My Restoration	"He restoreth my soul."
My Guidance	"He guideth me in the paths of righteousness for His Name's sake."
My Journey	"Yea, though I walk through the valley of the shadow of death."
My Courage	"I will fear no evil."
My Companion	"For Thou are with me."
My Comfort	"Thy rod and Thy staff, they comfort me."
My Provision	"Thou preparest a table before me."

My Victory	"In the presence of mine enemies."
My Anointing	"Thou hast anointed my head with oil."
My Abundance	"My cup runneth over."
My Attendants	"Goodness and mercy."
My Life	"All the days of my life."
My Eternity	"And I shall dwell in the house of Jehovah forever."

A speaker tested an audience of thousands by requesting them to repeat the Twenty-third Psalm. He was surprised and impressed by the great number who repeated it from memory. It is splendid to be among the millions who know the phraseology of the six-verse psalm; however, all its blessings are lost if one does not know the Shepherd of the psalm.

Friends honored a noted elocutionist and actor with a banquet. During the evening he was asked to give a reading; he chose the Twenty-third Psalm. His clean enunciation, delicate expression, and impressive phraseology caused enthusiastic applause. Later in the evening, a preacher 85 years of age was asked to speak; he read the Twenty-third Psalm. Everything about his reading evidenced heart-experience of the blessings assured in the psalm. When he concluded, there was no applause, but everyone seemed to be in tears. The elocutionist and actor, grasping his hand, said, "Sir, I know the psalm, but you know the Shepherd."

The great Shepherd described in Psalm 23 is the resurrected Lord and Saviour Jesus Christ. One can never know Him as Shepherd until they receive Him as Saviour. As Saviour and Shepherd, He will never fail to make real to the trusting soul in time and eternity the blessings assured in this psalm. He died as the Good Shepherd on Calvary's cross to secure these blessings for saved ones! He lives in His resurrected, crucified body as the Great Shepherd to impart these blessings to believers during their life on earth! He is coming a second time as the Chief Shepherd to fully culminate these blessings for every Christian! He is willing, faithful, and able!

During America's civil war, a little drummer lad was fatally wounded. An older soldier, who had promised to keep an eye on him, insisted upon sending word to his mother. She hastened to the military hospital, where doctors informed her that her boy's condition precluded all hope of his living; that he was in a stupor and if aroused he would experience paroxysms of pain. After much pleading, she was granted permission to sit by his side, upon promising that she would not speak a word to him. Sitting there, she noticed expressions on her boy's face that indicated intense suffering. Without saying a word, she leaned over and put her hand upon his brow. The dying soldier boy did not open his eyes, but she noticed his lips moving. Bending lower she heard him say repeatedly, "I knew you would come—I knew you would come—I knew you would come."

God's saved ones can be sure that in every disappointment, upset, sorrow, and trial during pilgrimage through this earth's night of sin and woe, they have a great Saviour and Shepherd who "has come." He is abundantly able and willing to minister to them with ability even surpassing that of a loving mother.

"Now the God of peace, that brought again from the dead our Lord Jesus, that great shepherd of the sheep, through the blood of the everlasting covenant, Make you perfect in every good work to do his will, working in you that which is wellpleasing in his sight, through Jesus Christ; to whom be glory for ever and ever. Amen." (Hebrews 13:20, 21).

Chapter 7

Plentitude

There are one hundred and eighteen words in the twenty-third psalm. They can be clearly and fully repeated in forty-five seconds. Yet this brief portion of Scripture presents a full scope of God's blessings for His redeemed ones during their temporal life on earth and their eternal life in glory. It also gives a full view of God's redemptive work for His own.

The number seven speaks of completion throughout the Bible. In natural and spiritual realms God completes His work in cycles of seven. His complete redemptive work for believers is described through seven references to Himself as Jehovah. The word "Lord" as used in verse 1 of Psalm 23 and elsewhere in the Old Testament, when studied in capitalized Hebrew language, is the same as *Jehovah*. The Scofield Reference Bible footnote on Genesis 2:4 states: "The primary meanings of the name Lord (Jehovah) is 'the self-existent one.' Literally, 'He that is who He is, therefore the eternal I am.' But Havah, from which Jehovah, or Yahwe, is formed, signifies also 'to become,' that is, to become known, thus pointing to a continuous and increasing self-revelation. Combining these meaning of Havah, we arrive at the meaning of the name Jehovah. He is 'the self-existent One who reveals Himself.'"

In the creation account in Genesis 1, the Hebrew word for God is *Elohim*; it is a uni-plural noun signifying power. It is significant that the name of God changes to "the Lord" or "Jehovah" after man is created, and especially after he has fallen in sin. It is the Lord God, or Jehovah-Elohim, who seeks man in his lost and fallen state (Genesis 3:8-13, 21). Jehovah is the redemption name of God. Jehovah of the Old Testament, who is always associated with God's redemptive work, is the Jesus of the New Testament through whom God's redemptive work is wrought and consummated.

In Exodus 3, the Lord God, meaning Jehovah God, revealed Himself to Moses when commissioning him to deliver His people from Egypt. This deliverance is a wondrous type of the redemption of God's children through Jesus Christ. While commissioning Moses, God named Himself, "I Am that I AM." This name of deity means "a living One who is, who was, and who is to come"; One who is eternally self-existent and thus ever abundantly sufficient for every situation; One who is continually revealed. Jesus Christ, in John 8:58, when asserting His deity, claimed to be this "I Am." For salvation He is the "I Am," meaning the One exclusively and entirely sufficient for it. He is the same for every temptation, trial, burden, sorrow, or experience on earth. He is also the exclusive and sufficient supply for everything needed for eternal, glorified life with God. The New Testament reveals that He is God's "I Am" in such statements as:

I am the Bread of life	John 6:35
I am the Light of the world	John 8:12
I am the Door of the sheep	John 10:7
I am the Door of salvation	John 10:9
I am the Good Shepherd	John 10:11
I am the true Vine	John 15:1
I am the Vine	John 15:5
I am the Resurrection and the Life	John 11:25
I am the Way, Truth, and Life	John 14:6
I am the Alpha and Omega, the Beginning and Ending, saith the Lord, which is, and was, and which is to come, the Almighty	Revelation 1:8, 22:13
I am the Root and Offspring of David	Revelation 22:16
I am the Bright and Morning Star	Revelation 22:16

One of God's redemptive names is *Jehovah-Raah*. In Psalm 23:1 it is translated, "The LORD is my Shepherd." How blessed to realize that the Shepherd of Psalm 23 is Jehovah, the Christian's Saviour, the Lord Jesus Christ; the One described as the **Good Shepherd,** who dies for His sheep (John 10:11); the **Great Shepherd,** who cares for His sheep (Hebrews 13:20); and the **Chief Shepherd,** who is coming for His sheep (I Peter 5:4). The Christian's perfect, omnipotent, omniscient, and omnipresent Shepherd; a divine Shepherd for every detail of His life from the beginning to the consummation of His salvation.

Another of Jehovah's compound redemptive names is *Jehovah-Jireh*. In Genesis 22:14, it is translated, "The LORD will provide." It was uttered by God's Spirit through Abraham on Mount Moriah. Isaac had said to his father, "Behold the fire and the wood: but where is the lamb for a burnt-offering?" And Abraham replied, "My son, God will provide himself a lamb for a burnt offering" (Genesis 22:7, 8). When God withheld Abraham's hand from slaying Isaac as a sacrifice and revealed a substitute ram caught in a thicket to be used as the sacrifice, Abraham called the name of the place "Jehovah-Jireh."

In verse 2 of Psalm 23 we see Jehovah, the Shepherd, fulfilling that which is indicated by the name Jehovah-Jireh. He provides sustenance for His sheep through green pastures and still waters. Throughout the New Testament, God assures Christians that through Christ, their Saviour and Shepherd, He is able to do exceeding abundant for them above all they can ask or think (Ephesians 3:20); also, that all their needs will be supplied according to His riches in glory by Christ Jesus (Philippians 4:19).

In Exodus 15:26, God refers to Himself as *Jehovah-Rapha*. Translated, it reads, "I am the LORD that healeth thee." In this chapter he healed the bitter waters through sweetening them. Jehovah continually heals mentally, physically, and spiritually. The expression, "He restoreth my soul," in verse 3 of this psalm refers to a work of God, through Jesus Christ the Shepherd, which involves mental, physical, and spiritual healing. Rescuing a lost sheep or restoring a straying one includes healing in these three respects.

> *There were ninety and nine that safely lay*
> *In the shelter of the fold,*
> *But one was out on the hills away,*
> *Far off from the gates of gold;*

Away on the mountains wild and bare,
   Away from the tender Shepherd's care.

But none of the ransomed ever knew
   How deep were the waters crossed;
Nor how dark was the night that the Lord passed thro'
   Ere He found His sheep that was lost.
Out in the desert He heard its cry—
   Sick and helpless, and ready to die.

But all through the mountains, thunder-riven,
   And up from the rocky steep,
There arose a cry to the gate of heaven,
   "Rejoice, I have found my sheep!"
And the angels echoed around the throne,
   "Rejoice, for the Lord brings back His own!"
("There Were Ninety and Nine That Safely Lay," Clephane, 1868)

Jesus Christ, the Jehovah of the Old Testament, healed the demoniac mentally (Mark 5:1-20); healed multitudes physically, even the leper (Mark 1 40-42); and healed many spiritually, especially when casting demons out of such as the Syrophenician woman's daughter (Matthew 15:22-28).

In Jeremiah 23:6 God is called *"Jehovah Tsidkenu."* It is translated, "THE LORD OUR RIGHTEOUSNESS." In Psalm 23, verse 3, we read of Jehovah, the Shepherd, leading His own into the paths of righteousness. The work of righteousness referred to in this verse is wrought through Jesus Christ, the Jehovah-Shepherd of the Old Testament.

In the New Testament, righteousness as related to Christians means words, thought, and acts which are right before God. Such living is possible only as Christ lives in and through believers (Romans 7:18, 8:3, 4).

There is also the righteousness of God which is credited to and placed upon all that believe in Christ Jesus (Romans 3:21-28). This righteousness is possible only through Jesus Christ. He hath been made righteousness unto all who receive Him as Saviour (I Corinthians 1:30). "For he [God] hath made him [Jesus] to be sin for us [sinners], who knew no sin; that we [believers] might be made the righteousness of God in him" (II Corinthians 5:21).

In Judges 6:24, God is referred to as *"Jehovah-Shalom."* Translated, it means, "The LORD our peace." Gideon used this name when returning to God in true worship. The nation Israel was in captivity to the Midians and had lost God's peace because of departure from His will.

In Psalm 23, verse 4, the peace of God is witnessed to in life and death. Such peace is impossible until one has peace with God. Jesus Christ, the Jehovah-Shepherd of Psalm 23, is the exclusive source and channel of God's peace. He declared such when stating, "Peace I leave with you, my peace I give unto you; not as the world giveth, give I unto you. Let not your heart be troubled, neither let it be afraid" (John 14:27). He made peace through the blood of His cross (Colossians 1:20). "Therefore being justified by faith, we have peace with God through our Lord Jesus Christ" (Romans 5:1). Again God's Word says, "The peace of God, which passeth all understanding, shall keep [garrison] your hearts and minds through Christ Jesus" (Philippians 4:7). Surely Jesus Christ is God's peace for God's child (Ephesians 2:14).

This present world, so full of darkness, doubt, despair, defeat, destruction, and death, will never have peace apart from Jesus Christ, the Prince of Peace. His is this world's great need. God states that the wicked (unsaved) are like the troubled sea whose waters cast upon mire and dirt, and that there is no peace to the wicked (Isaiah 57:20, 21). In Job God says, "Acquaint now thyself with him, and be at peace" (Job 22:21). One cannot enjoy the peace of God until he has come to know Him, and one can only acquaint himself with God through Christ because He is the way, the truth, and the life and no man cometh unto the Father but by Him (John 14:6). God's Word emphatically declares that "this is life eternal, that they might know thee the only true God, and Jesus Christ, whom thou hast sent" (John 17:3).

God is addressed as *"Jehovah-Nissi"* in Exodus 17:15. Translated it reads, "The LORD our banner." It is associated with victory made possible by God. It was stated by Moses while worshipping God because of Israel's victory over Amalek. Amalek was a descendent of Esau and illustrates the flesh.

The fifth verse of Psalm 23, where God's prepared table, anointing oil, and overflowing cup are experienced by His people in the midst of enemies, describes the work of Jehovah-Nissi in imparting victory. All God's victories for saved ones are made possible through Jesus Christ, the Jehovah-Saviour and Shepherd of God's people. In Him saved ones have victory over the working force of sin within themselves, also over the flesh, the world, and Satan (Romans 8:2-4). When assailed by tribulation, distress, persecution, famine, nakedness, peril, or sword, they are more than conquerors through Christ Jesus (Romans 8:37). Facing death, they triumphantly cry, "O death, where is thy sting? O grave, where is thy victory? The sting of death is sin; and the strength of sin is the law. But thanks be to God, which giveth us the victory through our Lord Jesus Christ" (I Corinthians 15:55-57). Jesus Christ, the Jehovah-Shepherd of Psalm 23, fulfills the work of Jehovah-Nissi described in this psalm. "Now thanks be unto God, which always causeth us to triumph in Christ, and maketh manifest the savour of his knowledge by us in every place" (II Corinthians 2:14).

The book of Ezekiel closes with the words, "The LORD is there" (Ezekiel 48:35). In the Hebrew the name is *"Jehovah-Shammah."* This compound name assures the presence of the Lord. In Psalm 23, verse 6, a saved one dwells forever in the presence of the Lord. His presence assures all needed power, protection, provision, blessedness, victory, and glory. David, through whom God wrote Psalm 23, declared that in God's presence there is fullness of joy (Psalm 16:11).

The blessings because of Jehovah-Shammah, and described in this last verse of the psalm, are fulfilled through Jesus Christ, who is God of very God, and who said, "lo, I am with you always, even unto the end of the world" (Matthew 28:20); also, "I will never leave thee, nor forsake thee" (Hebrews 13:5), thus assuring every Christian of the Godhead's presence and consequent blessings during temporal life on earth and eternal life in heaven.

Krikorian, in his book on the Twenty-third Psalm, tells of a little Armenian orphan boy named Daveed Doonian who, while too young to talk, was found toddling about alone and with a diseased, filthy body during First World War days. Kind hands and hearts so ministered as to cleanse, clothe, and heal his body. As days went by, he entwined himself about the heartstrings of those who befriended him. At night he slept on the floor of a tent by the side of a woman who was paid to mother and shepherd him. Often he would awaken in the darkness of night in deadly fear because of the growl or bark of a dog. With only the cloth of the tent between him and the dogs, his little hand would reach out until it touched the kind woman, and a small voice whispered, *"Marrik* [the Armenian word for mother], is your face toward me now?" When he was assured that his *marrik's* (mother's) face was toward him, he would fall into restful sleep

(M. P. Krikorian, *The Spirit of the Shepherd: An Interpretation of the Psalm Immortal,* 1950).

How blessed the message of this psalm, which assures every saved one that God's face is toward them during every dark and bright experience of life on earth. How much more blessed its assurance that following life on earth they shall forever gaze into the face of their Redeemer, Saviour, Shepherd, and God without a thing, not even a veil of darkness, between.

A Navajo Indian, who gave genuine evidence of having received Jesus Christ as Saviour and thus experienced His Shepherd care, translated this psalm from his Navajo language into English. The translation reads:

> The great Father above is a Shepherd Chief, and I am His, and with Him I want not. He throws out to me a rope, and the name of the rope is love. He draws me, and He draws me, and He draws me to where the grass is green, and the water is not dangerous, and I eat and lie down satisfied.
>
> Sometimes my heart is very weak, and falls down, but He lifts it up again, and draws me into a good road. His name is Wonderful. Sometime—it may be very soon, it may be longer, it may be a long, long time—He will draw me into a place between mountains. It is dark there, but I will not draw back: I will not be afraid, for it is in there between these mountains that the Shepherd Chief will meet me, and the hunger I have felt in my heart all through this life will be satisfied. Sometimes He makes the love rope into a whip, but afterwards He gives me a staff to lean upon.
>
> He spreads a table before me with all kinds of food. He puts His hand upon my head, and all "tired" is gone. My cup He fills it till it runs over.

How comforting, wonderful, and yet challenging to know that God offers to be all that is indicated by His seven compound redemptive names—**Jehovah-Raah, Jehovah-Jireh, Jehovah-Rapha, Jehovah-Tsidkenu, Jehovah-Shalom, Jehovah-Nissi,** and **Jehovah-Shammah**—to every individual who receives Jesus Christ as Saviour. Whosoever will, may do so.

A missionary in London placed a sixpence on a table before three hundred boys and said, "Whosoever will come and take the sixpence can have it. "One of the three hundred boys walked forward and took the coin. The speaker asked, "What is your name?" The little fellow said, "Cecil Smithers." The missionary said, "I did not say that if Cecil Smithers came and took the sixpence he could have it." The little fellow replied, "No, you did not say my name, but you did say 'whosoever will' and that meant me." There were three hundred "whosoevers" in the room who heard the offer. There was only one "whosoever will." He acted and received the money.

The riches of Psalm 23 await anyone who will trust in Jesus Christ's shed blood, death, and resurrection to atone for their sin and save their soul. By this definite act of faith, they receive Jesus Christ as Saviour and He becomes their Shepherd. Without that definite act of faith, they reject Him as Saviour and thus miss His Shepherd blessings.

What I tell you is true, I lie not. These roads that are away ahead will stay with me through this life; and afterward I will go to live in the big tepee, and sit down with the Shepherd Chief forever.

Study Questions

Chapter 1

1. What is the three-fold aspect of how Scripture presents Christ as Shepherd?
2. Psalm 23 magnifies the work of our Shepherd/Saviour during our _____ _____ _____.
3. What is a *pilgrim*? Discuss characteristics of a pilgrim. Describe how you are living as a pilgrim, or, if your focus is on the things of this life, what adjustments you need to make in order to live like a pilgrim.
4. Who is the human author of Psalm 23 through which the Holy Spirit spoke?
5. What is the most vital word in verse 1?
6. What do the words "not want" in verse 1 assure us of?
7. Discuss the comparison between the temporary sufficiency of earthly things and the permanent sufficiency of eternal truth.

Chapter 2

8. Why is Psalm 23 called "the nightingale song"?
9. What does "lying down" refer to?

10. Discuss times in your life when, through circumstances or self-failure, you have been brought to the point of "lying down" before the Lord. What were the lessons you learned?
11. What are good New Testament verses to meditate on during our times of "lying down"?
12. How does our Shepherd/Saviour lead us along?
13. Discuss how you are currently building a resource of Scripture into your life (e.g., meditating, memorizing, etc.).

Chapter 3

14. Where does the fullness of the Godhead bodily dwell?
15. How do we become a sheep?
16. What is not affected when a sheep strays?
17. What is affected when a sheep strays?
18. When we accept Jesus Christ as our Saviour, what do we possess?
19. In light of this truth, turn in the New Testament to Romans 5 and in observing verses 1-11, list what you practically possess because of your positional possession of God's righteousness.
20. What are the two chief pronouns in verse 3?

Chapter 4

21. How is death referred to for the believer?
22. Give two descriptions of the answer to question 1.
23. Discuss times in your life when, as a child, a shadow of something brought fear to you, but as you grew older you realized the harmlessness of it. Describe how you would apply this to your spiritual growth.
24. What three things does God's presence assure us of?

Chapter 5

25. In the Bible, what does every text lead to?
26. What does oil symbolize?
27. What is the Holy Spirit's three-fold ministry?
28. Read and meditate on Galatians 5:13-26 in the New Testament. Examine whether or not in your life you are manifesting self-control or spirit-control. Describe which areas you need to submit to the Spirit's control.
29. What did Christ drink so that we can enjoy the overflowing cup of verse 5?

Chapter 6

30. What are the "sweet 'P's" of Psalm 23?
31. How is the believer in Christ portrayed in verse 6?
32. Why is the first word in verse 6 so important?
33. Discuss the difference between basing your assurance on your feelings versus basing your assurance on the truth of the Word of God. Describe how Satan has used your feelings to rob you of assurance in the past and how you can confess the truth of Scripture in the future to resist these attacks.
34. How many personal pronouns are there in Psalm 23?
35. Describe specific areas of your life where you can personally apply these 27 truths.

Chapter 7

36. Jehovah is the _____ name of God.
37. Jehovah of the Old Testament is the _____ of the New Testament.
38. What title did Jesus use in the New Testament to show His Deity?
39. Define the compound redemptive names of God that apply to Psalm 23:
    a. Jehovah-Roah
    b. Jehovah-Jireh
    c. Jehovah-Rapha
    d. Jehovah-Tsidkenu
    e. Jehovah-Shalom
    f. Jehovah-Nissi
    g. Jehovah-Shammah
40. Memorize the preceding list and specifically share particular needs in your current life in which these personal names can be claimed and applied.

Study Answers

Chapter 1
1. Good-Great-Shepherd.
2. pilgrimage on earth.
3. [Answers will vary.]
4. David.
5. "my." Based on John 3 in the New Testament, why I can say with assurance that Christ is my Saviour.
6. Total sufficiency of our Saviour/Shepherd.
7. [Answers will vary.]

Chapter 2
8. Because the nightingale sings in the night.
9. Humility.
10. [Answers will vary.]
11. Romans 8:28 30.
12. Indwelling Holy Spirit leads through the Scripture.
13. [Answers will vary.]

Chapter 3

14. In Christ.
15. Saved from sin/ruin.
16. Relationship.
17. Fellowship.
18. God's righteousness.
19. [Answers will vary.]
20. "He" and "me."

Chapter 4

21. As a shadow.
22. Shadows are harmless and temporary.
23. [Answers will vary.]
24. Provision, protection, power.

Chapter 5

25. Jesus Christ.
26. Holy Spirit.
27. Indwells/anoints/fills.
28. [Answers will vary.]
29. Cup of sin/death/hell.

Chapter 6

30. Possession/position/promise/progress/provision/prospect.
31. Dweller/house/Lord.
32. Assurance; [answers will vary.]
33. [Answers will vary.]
34. 27.
35. [Answers will vary.]

Chapter 7

36. redemptive.
37. Jesus.
38. I Am.
39.
    a. Jehovah-Roah—*Shepherd*
    b. Jehovah-Jireh—*Provider*
    c. Jehovah-Rapha—*Healer*
    d. Jehovah-Tsidkenu—*Righteousness*
    e. Jehovah-Shalom—*Peace*

f. Jehovah-Nissi—*Victory*
   g. Jehovah-Shammah—*Presence*
40. [Answers will vary.]

The Authors

DR. WILLIAM MCCARRELL
February 8, 1886 – August 25, 1979

Dr. William "Billy" McCarrell was born in Chicago to Samuel and Sarah McCarrell. After a rocky childhood and youth, McCarrell graduated from Moody Bible Institute. He served as pastor of the First Congregational Church of Cicero which later changed its name to Cicero Bible Church. During his forty-five years at the church, he saw growth from a congregation of twenty-five to an average attendance in Sunday school and church between nine hundred and one thousand—a

megachurch in its time. He saw the church through prosperity and depression and through two world wars.

The church supported hundreds of missionaries around the world and McCarrell helped plant twenty churches in the Chicago area. He also oversaw weekly radio broadcasts on WGN radio as well as The Moody Network. The Fisherman's Club, a weekly evangelistic outreach of men to the Chicago area, was founded by McCarrell. Records kept by the church show some amazing facts:

- 533,815 people were dealt with concerning salvation and eternal destiny.
- 140,000 professions of faith in Christ were recorded.
- 17,159,690 gospel tracts were passed out.
- Daily radio broadcasts were beamed out over five stations, including WGN.
- The Cicero Press was established (1923) for the purpose of producing good Christian books and literature; eventually it was sold to a large publisher and moved out of Cicero.
- 250 Christian workers were sent out, influenced by Cicero Bible Church.
- The very first bus ministry in America was organized, picking up entire families and bringing them to Sunday school and church services at Cicero Bible Church. The bus ministry continued even during the gas-rationing WWII years.

Wheaton College conferred an honorary doctorate on McCarrell, who served as a trustee on the board of Wheaton College for forty-nine years. At his funeral in 1979, the then-presiding president of Wheaton, Dr. Amerding, spoke of McCarrell's service and shared that with forty-six years of service, he was the longest serving trustee. While pastoring, he also served for twenty-two years as Professor of Local Church and Personal Evangelism at Moody Bible Institute. He also lectured at Dallas Theological Seminary, teaching on dispensationalism and church planting. This was during the presidency of Dr. John Walvoord, who was the spiritual son of Dr. McCarrell. In 1929, he founded an independent fellowship of churches (IFCA) along with his close friends Dr. M. R. DeHaan (Radio Bible Class), Dr. Oliver Buswell (president of Wheaton), and layman O. B. Bottorff.

After his retirement from Cicero Bible Church in 1958, he continued the work tirelessly, traveling across the country and to the

United Kingdom. A men's dormitory at Appalachian Bible College was named for him. He even pastored a church in Wisconsin for a time. Through the years, he served on more than fifty organizations, boards, and councils by providing administrative support, advice, or encouragement. They include Pacific Garden Mission, Faith Theological Seminary, Bryan College, Chicago Hebrew Mission, Great Commission Prayer League, and Lightbearer's Association.

McCarrell and his wife Minnie were the parents of nine children; their son Paul was killed in action during World War II. McCarrell was known as a "man of one Book" with a relentless evangelistic heart, always sharing Christ with those with whom he came in contact. He was known for his uncompromising stand for separation from the world.

Rev. Richard McCarrell

Rev. Rich McCarrell was born in 1954 and came to faith in Christ at the age of twelve under the ministry of Dr. Jack Murray of Bible Evangelism. Rich grew up attending Des Plaines Bible Church with Pastor Craig Massey in the western suburbs of Chicago for many years. Educated at Grand Rapids School of the Bible and Music, Appalachian Bible College, and Frontier Bible College, Rich also has an honorary doctorate conferred by Calvary Bible College and Seminary in Kansas City.

Rich has been involved in local church ministry since 1976 as youth pastor, associate pastor, and as senior pastor for the past thirty-six years in Michigan and Philadelphia. He served on a variety of mission boards, led two study tours of Israel, and been involved in multiple international trips visiting missionaries and training national pastors in Indonesia, India, and Haiti.

Rich and Sue were married in 1975 after meeting in college. They currently reside in the Grand Rapids, Michigan, area where Rich continues to serve as senior pastor. They are the parents of two married children and grandparents to three.

If you liked Shepherd, we think you'll also like:

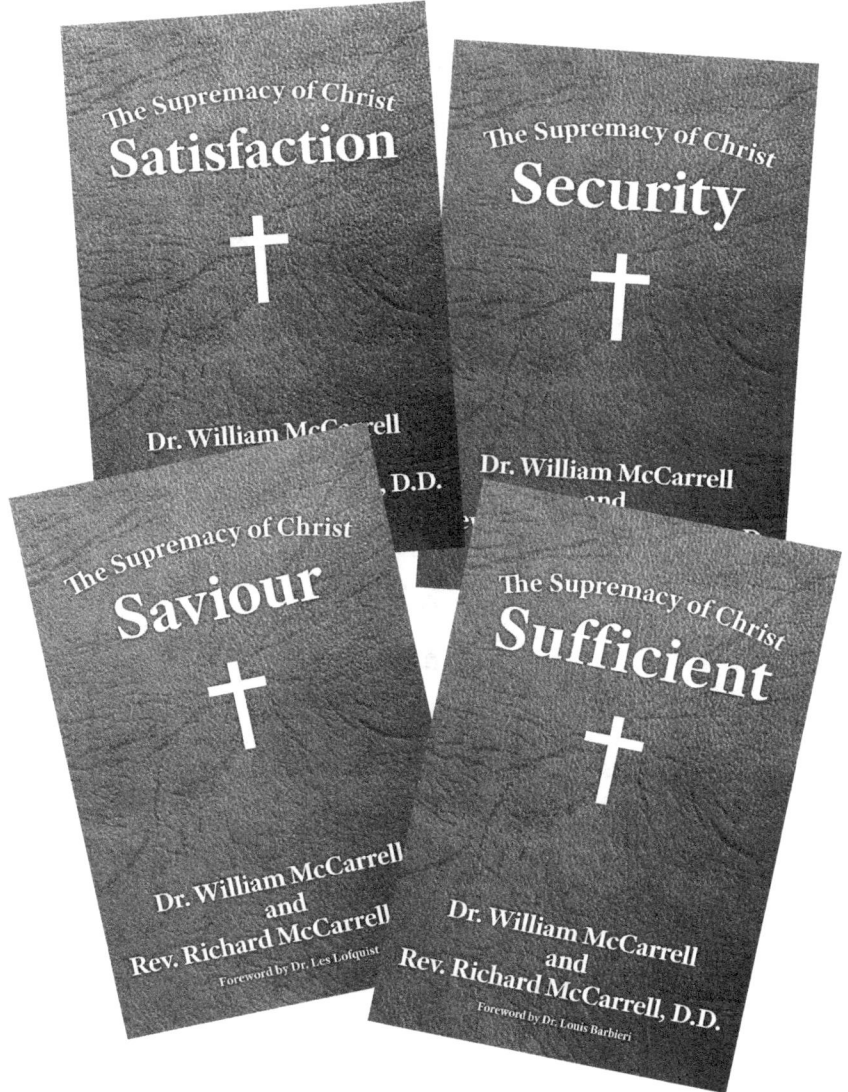

Available at GraceAcresPress.com or your favorite bookseller.

Growing Your Faith
One Page at a Time

Print, video, and speaker solutions
for churches, small groups,
organizations, and individuals.

GraceAcresPress.com

303-681-9995

www.ingramcontent.com/pod-product-compliance
Lightning Source LLC
Chambersburg PA
CBHW052122070526
44586CB00016B/2048